D1569514

CHILDREN OF DIVORCE
A Practical Guide for Parents, Therapists,
Attorneys, and Judges

CHILDREN OF DIVORCE
A Practical Guide for Parents, Therapists, Attorneys, and Judges

Second Edition

William Bernet, M.D.

Professor in the Department of Psychiatry
Director, Vanderbilt Forensic Services
Vanderbilt University School of Medicine, Nashville, Tennessee

Don R. Ash, J.D., M.J.S.

Circuit Court Judge
Sixteenth Judicial District of Tennessee
Murfreesboro, Tennessee

KRIEGR PUBLISHING COMPANY
Malabar, Florida
2007

Second Edition 2007

Printed and Published by
KRIEGER PUBLISHING COMPANY
KRIEGER DRIVE
MALABAR, FLORIDA 32950

**FROM A DECLARATION OF PRINCIPLES JOINTLY ADOPTED BY A COM-
MITTEE OF THE AMERICAN BAR ASSOCIATION AND A COMMITTEE
OF PUBLISHERS:**
This publication is designed to provide accurate and authoritative information
in regard to the subject matter covered. It is sold with the understanding that
the publisher is not engaged in rendering legal, accounting, or other
professional service. If legal advice or other expert assistance is required, the
services of a competent professional person should be sought.

Library of Congress Cataloging-in-Publication Data

Bernet, William.
  Children of divorce : a practical guide for parents, therapists, attorneys, and
judges / William Bernet, Don R. Ash. — 2nd ed.
      p. cm.
Includes bibliographical references and index.
ISBN-13: 978-1-57524-288-0 (alk. paper)
ISBN-10: 1-57524-288-5 (alk. paper)
1. Children of divorced parents—United States. 2. Children of divorced
parents—United States—Psychology. 3. Custody of children—United States.
I. Ash, Don R., 1935- II. Title.
  HQ777.5.B49 2007
  306.89—dc22

                                                           2007012527

10 9 8 7 6 5 4 3 2

Contents

Introduction

This book fills an important need. Many books about parenting are available that cover every period of life from infancy to the developmental stage of adult children still living at home. Individuals who are getting divorced may consult many self-help books, web sites, and support groups, which help people deal with their feelings of anger, loss, and loneliness. Therapists treating divorced individuals and their children may refer to professional books. There is not so much available for divorced parents who are trying hard to nurture their children. Raising the children of divorce is a challenging task. When divorced parents organize their list of priorities, raising their children may fall below having a full-time job and trying to reestablish social relationships.

Children of Divorce is intended for several audiences. It is primarily intended for parents who are divorcing or already divorced and are hoping to rear their children in a healthy manner. *Children of Divorce* is also intended for legal professionals, both attorneys and judges, since they help shape the lives of the children of divorce. We think attorneys and judges will find some of our suggestions to be unusual, but innovative and useful. This book is also for other persons who love or work with children of divorced families including grandparents, relatives, therapists, and school personnel. Although this is not a technical treatise, this book contains many discussions and suggestions that therapists, counselors, and teachers should find helpful.

Children of Divorce focuses on two issues: what to do about conflict and how to provide the maximum amount of stability. Our underlying premise is that children of divorce are injured by the lack of stability in their lives, but especially by the continuing conflict between their parents. This book does not dwell on the problems, but emphasizes solutions. It offers many ways to minimize the conflict that children of divorce experience day-in and day-out. Many of the suggestions in *Children of Divorce* are very easy to bring about and could be implemented independently by either the custodial parent (now called the "primary residential parent") or the noncustodial parent (now called the "non-primary residential parent"). Some of the suggestions are more complicated and require the active cooperation of both parents. A few of them, such as suggestions in the chapter about "Uncommon Custody Arrangements," might require attorneys and the action of a judge.

Getting divorced is not a rose garden. The divorce presumably came about as a way to resolve difficulties between the couple, but it creates a whole new set of issues. In particular, it creates a challenge for the mother and father, who now dislike each other very much, to discover new ways to cooperate in raising the children. There are no easy answers. Simplistic solutions are not usually much help because every divorced family has its own particular nuances and requirements. We will present, however, important general principles and many specific suggestions that divorced parents should find usable and practical.

Psychology and Law

The ideas in this book have been derived from many sources including personal experiences with our families and conversations with friends and colleagues who have been divorced. Our careers as a child psychiatrist and as a judge have allowed us to meet and treat many children of divorce and their parents. As you will see, the psychological material and the legal material has been blended into chapters that should make sense to both mental health and legal professionals, but still be pertinent for the typical adult reader.

When child development topics and mental health issues are addressed in *Children of Divorce*, we are relying on mainstream child psychiatry and child psychology. While psychiatrists and psychologists may disagree on some of the details, there is fundamental agreement on basic notions such as the importance of having a good relationship with both parents, the importance of stability, and the harmful nature of domestic violence and family feuding.

The adults who care for and interact with children of divorce must take laws and legal facts of life into consideration. These laws vary from state to state. Although general legal principles are uniform throughout this country, individual states may be inconsistent or even flatly disagree among themselves when it comes to the details. This is not a basic textbook of family law, but we have included summaries of a number of important legal cases. These "reported" or published cases—from appellate courts, state supreme courts, and the U.S. Supreme Court—usually set precedents that other courts subsequently followed.

We included these cases not just for the benefit of attorneys and judges, but also for the nonprofessional reader. These legal cases are sometimes quite poignant and the situations will sound familiar to divorced parents. Also, these cases are intended to help the nonprofessional reader understand where the "rules" come from that control legal decisions. We hope that these cases convey something about the way individual judges and groups of judges—such as appellate courts—think about these troublesome family situations. In the end, we have based our suggestions regarding children of divorce on three funds of knowledge: our experience and practical knowledge of what good-hearted people want for their children; concepts of normal and abnormal child development; and laws and legal precedents. These laws and precedents provide both guideposts and boundaries in this difficult terrain.

Case material—both clinical and legal—is frequently mentioned in this book. In reported legal cases, the names and circumstances of the family are already public knowledge. With regard to unreported legal cases and all clinical material, names and other details have been changed to protect the individual's identity and the family's confidentiality. At times, two or more actual families have been blended or merged into one narrative in order to illustrate some concept or lesson.

Terminology

In the first edition of this book, divorced parents were referred to as the "custodial parent" and the "noncustodial parent." Of course, that was standard terminology for many years and still is in some jurisdictions. However, some states have passed laws emphasizing that children of divorce should be nurtured and raised by both parents. In order to get away from the notion that the custodial parent was totally in charge and the noncustodial parent was a second-class citizen, state legislators have emphasized shared parenting. For too many years not only families, but our legal system has treated children like personal property. In an environment when almost fifty percent of all marriages end in divorce, we must try to build a foundation for both parents to participate in the development of the children.

Rather than refer to custodial and noncustodial parents, the newer state laws use terms such as "primary residential parent" and "nonprimary residential parent." At least one state (Tennessee) has introduced the term "alternate residential parent" for the person who is not the primary residential parent. Although these terms are cumbersome, we feel there are many advantages to this change in focus from disputes over custody to developing a plan for shared parenting. With this in mind, we will attempt to avoid the use of terms like "custody" and "visitation." Instead, we will use terms such as "residential parenting," "parenting plans," and "co-parenting." We will ordinarily use the terms "primary residential parent" (abbreviated "PRP") and "nonprimary residential parent" ("NPRP"). In some chapters and in some contexts, however, it still makes sense to refer to the "custodial" and "noncustodial" parent, so both sets of terms appear in *Children of Divorce.*

We have attempted to make this book gender-neutral. For example, sometimes the custodial parent is referred to as "he" and sometimes as "she." Likewise, the child in one example might be referred to as "he" and in another example as "she."

Thank You's

In working on this project, we have enjoyed the support and appreciated the suggestions of our wives, Susan Bernet and Rita Ash. Dr. Bernet's children and stepchildren—Henry, Alice, Daniel, and Elizabeth—provided some of the examples used in the book. Judge Ash's children—Julia, Hugh, Taylor, and Joy—have been both helpful and wise.

We thank colleagues and friends for their comments and constructive criticism. Linda Wirth, ACSW, Ms. Johanna Stein, and Diane Schetky, M.D., read earlier versions of *Children of Divorce* and made helpful suggestions. James S. Walker, Ph.D., read the manuscript and helped us clarify sections that were ambiguous or unclear. Caroline D.S. Piggott, M.D., helped develop the chapter on Internet resources regarding children of divorce. Our assistants, Cheryl McDonald and Amanda DeLisle in Nashville and Michelle Blaylock-Houser in Murfreesboro, were supportive and helped manage the details of our work.

William Bernet, M.D.   Judge Don R. Ash, J.D., M.J.S.
Nashville, Tennessee   Murfreesboro, Tennessee

Chapter One
Basic Strategies

Then there came two women, that were harlots, to the king, and stood before him; and one of them said: I beseech thee, my lord, I and this woman dwelt in one house, and I was delivered of a child with her in the chamber. And the third day, after that I was delivered, she also was delivered, and we were together, and no other person with us in the house, only we two. And this woman's child died in the night, for in her sleep she overlaid him. And rising in the dead time of the night, she took my child from my side, while I thy handmaid was asleep, and laid it in her bosom, and laid her dead child in my bosom. And when I rose in the morning to give my child suck, behold it was dead, but considering him more diligently when it was clear day, I found that it was not mine which I bore. And the other woman answered: It is not so as thou sayest, but thy child is dead, and mine is alive. On the contrary she said: Thou liest, for my child liveth, and thy child is dead. And in this manner they strove before the king.

Then said the king: The one saith: My child is alive, and thy child is dead. And the other answereth: Nay, but thy child is dead, and mine liveth. The king therefore said: Bring me a sword. And when they had brought a sword before the king: Divide, said he, the living child in two, and give half to the one, and half to the other. But the woman whose child was alive, said to the king (for her bowels were moved upon her child): I beseech thee, my lord, give her the child alive, and do not kill it. But the other said: Let it be neither mine nor thine, but divide it. The king answered, and said: Give the living child to this woman, and let it not be killed, for she is the mother thereof.

And all Israel heard the judgment which the king had judged, and they feared the king, seeing that the wisdom of God was in him to do judgment.

1 Kings 3:16-28

The timeless story of Solomon from the First Book of Kings continues to send powerful messages for divorced parents and their children. The basic plot is reenacted hundreds and thousands of times in every city: it is the story of two adults disputing their right to a child; the dilemma of the judge attempting to determine which adult is truly more worthy to take the child; and the baby who is being destroyed in the process. Another motif is the woman—presumably the true mother— who was trying to balance her own right to the baby with the baby's right to stay in one piece and survive the custody dispute. In the story of Solomon, the true mother decided the baby's right to life was stronger than her own right to possess the baby.

Parents and judges should not take the story of Solomon literally. Today, however, Solomon's order to cut the baby in half may be a metaphor for court-ordered joint custody. The outcome looks the same, in that neither parent is really pleased with the court's decision and the child suffers. Also, it may be that the parent who is willing to give up some control, by ensuring that the child maintain a good relationship with the other parent, is the preferred custodial or primary residential parent. Parents should think about the long-term welfare of their children instead of who is in control. This type of arrangement—court-ordered joint custody—will not work unless both parents are committed to work together. How does this happen? The parents must focus on the love they feel for their child instead of the anger and disappointment they feel toward each other.

It is hard to imagine how much suffering is experienced by the children of divorced parents. It starts during the marriage itself, when the child is aware of the disagreements and fighting between the parents. When one parent angrily packs up and moves out of the family home, the child may be confused and frightened. A child may experience a time of disbelief when she knows in her mind that her parents are splitting up, but does not accept it in her heart. Her suffering continues after the divorce, as she is whipsawed from one household to another and from one relationship to another.

We are not saying that every child of divorced parents has been damaged by the events related to his parents' splitting up. Many times, the children benefit from the divorce because it brings an end to the most severe level of fighting and, perhaps, even spousal abuse. Some children make the best of the divorce and the parents' subsequent marriages and thrive in the two newly created households. Generally, however, it is harder to grow up in two households than in one, intact, nurturing family. Even the lucky children—whose divorced parents collaborate and cooperate—carry with them into adulthood the stresses and strains of growing up in a divided family.

Since the process of separation and divorce will not disappear at any time in the foreseeable future, there is no way to completely protect our children from the consequences, but it should be possible to identify the major causes of distress for the children of divorce and to minimize their impact. Every family situation will have its own idiosyncrasies. However, we propose general guidelines for parents who are divorcing, which are intended to minimize the pain and the damage to the children. The general guidelines are: (1) Children of divorce should have a good relationship with both parents; (2) Divorced parents should find ways to minimize the disruptions and make life as normal as possible for their children; (3) Divorced parents and their children need to accept the inevitable losses and disappointments and move on with their lives.

The basic principles for raising children of divorce—which form the foundation for the rest of the book—are explained in this chapter. These principles are easy to explain, but parents may find them hard to follow. It is easier to be jealous and angry. Subsequent chapters will provide specific methods for minimizing the suffering of the children of divorce. There is no way to completely eliminate their suffering, but it should be possible to lighten the burden of these children.

1. Children of divorce should have a good relationship with both parents.

It is not always possible to achieve this goal. Sometimes the circumstances of life prevent a child from knowing or enjoying both parents. One or both of the parents may have died, abandoned the child, been abusive, or sustained a chronic illness that required the parent and the child to be apart from each other. One of the parents may be in prison and his or her parental rights were terminated.

In most divorces, however, there are two parents who should be able to develop and maintain a healthy, mutually satisfying relationship with the child. The biggest factor that prevents a child from having a good relationship with both parents is the amount of arguing and fighting between the parents. Bickering is a choice made by the parents, not the child. Although divorce is difficult for children to accept, they continue to love both parents. Parents who fight for the exclusive affection of their child will not only hurt themselves, but set up a foundation of failure for the child.

There are many aspects of parental separation and divorce that pain the children. The long list of potential hurts includes: the sense of uncertainty and insecurity because the family is not going to be together the way it used to be; the embarrassment when friends find out about the parents' divorce; the prospect of moving several times before the PRP settles down again; the daily and weekly disruptions to everyday life as the child shuttles from one household to the other; the loss of the NPRP as he or she drifts farther out of the child's life; and the inevitable financial hardships, because it costs more for divorced families to live in two households than it did for the intact family to live together. (PRP and NPRP refer to the "primary residential parent" and the "nonprimary residential parent." See page 4 for an explanation of the abbreviations.)

Of all the things that hurt when parents divorce, the part that aches the most is the fighting. Divorced parents fight in every which way. They fight *over the children* in custody disputes that may go on for years. In these disputes, the grown-ups discuss the failures of the other parent and his or her family. They fight *through the children* by using them as the carriers of parental vindictiveness, such as including the children in discussions of parenting times and financial needs. And they fight *in front of the children,* especially when the children are passing from one household to the other at the beginning and end of visitation. By the way, divorced parents do not have a monopoly on fighting in front of the children. Angry displays between married parents are also damaging to the children of intact families. While the parents may suffer during these disputes, it is the children who will carry this emotional baggage with them forever.

If divorcing parents were willing to hear and accept one piece of advice, it should be, "Don't fight with your former spouse." Of course, that advice is easy to give and extremely hard to accept. It is a suggestion that divorced parents always agree is absolutely correct, but the perception is that the *other parent* is always to blame. If parents were able to take this advice and put it into action, the children would stand a much better chance of having a happy and satisfying relationship with both the mother and the father. Relationships between the children and both parents would flourish with increased child support, better communication between the parents, and a willingness to raise together a well-adjusted child.

Divorce Statistics

This book does not have very many statistics, but here are a few. Almost one-half of all marriages in the United States end in divorce. That means approximately half of all children will spend some time in a single-parent household. Since half of the divorces occur before the seventh year of marriage, there are many divorced parents with young children. Each year about one million children experience the divorce of their parents. If you happen to want more statistics, refer to the National Center for Health Statistics, the nation's principal health statistics agency, at www.cdc.gov/nchs/.

The fact is two individuals who once were in love are not going to give each other up without a certain amount of fighting. If they really did care about each other when they were together, they are bound to experience anger, frustration, and resentment when they split up. Many times hearts are broken and trusts are violated. Rejection by a partner is a devastating life event. What really matters, of course, is that angry ex-spouses should exclude the children from the fighting. If you have some serious issue to discuss with your former partner, do it when the kids are in school. Try not to make your children into weapons of mass destruction. These topics are discussed in Chapter Two, "Fighting and the Children."

2. Divorced parents should find ways to minimize the disruptions and make life as normal as possible for their children.

Even children in normal, intact families can become stressed by their confusing, frantic schedules before school, during school, after school, and in the evenings. Our busy, harried children maintain calendars more complex than those of many adults. Their schedules are comparable to those of traveling salesmen. During the course of a week, children must deal with multiple teachers, car pools, bus drivers, and a variety of athletic, musical, and religious extracurricular activities. If both parents work, the children's lives become more complicated because they may spend part of the day in child care programs before and after school or they may experience a parade of other caretakers such as babysitters and grandparents. Remember, in this paragraph we are talking about children of intact families.

If the parents are divorced, the scheduling process can get out of control. The two parents may find it more convenient for themselves to make different day care and babysitting arrangements. As a result, that part of the child's life does not have a sense of continuity. If the child lives part of the week in one home and part in another, he may never completely unpack and unwind before moving on. Can you imagine what happens to a child's sense of identity and wholeness when his mother on her weekend takes him to art class and to Sunday school at the Church of Christ, but the father on his weekends signs the boy up for baseball and Catholic religious education? It is not a happy experience.

The solution is for divorced parents to put some thought into how to help the child carry on with his own life in a way that is predictable, consistent, and minimally disrupted by the needs of the parents. Parents should focus on the well-being of the child instead of the convenience for the parents' schedules. Making life reasonably routine and normal for these children requires several ingredients. It means, for instance, the parents should try to agree on matters such as the child's participation in organized sports teams, the child's medical care, and his religious upbringing. It means the parents should communicate regarding the most important household rules and policies in order for discipline to be fairly consistent in the two homes. It means divorced parents should agree on details such as the celebration of major holidays so that the child is not expected to sit through two Thanksgiving dinners on the same afternoon. Children need stability. This stability is not limited to where they sleep at night, but should extend to the feeling that the two adults who love them the most in the world will strive to make their childhood a dream rather than a nightmare.

This book contains many suggestions for ways to normalize the lives of the children of divorce. The chapters pertaining to that issue most directly are: Chapter Nine, "Living In Two Homes"; Chapter Ten, "Making Parenting Time Work"; Chapter Eleven, "Holidays and Holy Days"; and Chapter Thirteen, "Parental Rights and Responsibilities." Some states have adopted the use of parenting plans through which divorcing parents are expected to negotiate many of these issues before the divorce is finalized. This topic is discussed in Chapter Six, "Parenting Education and Parenting Plans."

3. Divorced parents and their children need to accept the inevitable losses and disappointments and move on with their lives.

There are many necessary losses that both children and parents must accept when divorce occurs. For instance, the children will have to give up the notion that their parents will get back together again and they will be one happy family. This is a common idea that children express, even after one or both parents have married again. The children need to give up the old homestead and community and be prepared to move to new surroundings. Even when the divorce goes smoothly, the children may not have the same intimacy and the same wealth of shared experiences with each parent.

The divorcing parents also need to acknowledge and accept important losses. Divorced parents usually have to manage on a tighter budget than when they were married. They have to give up the conveniences of a two-income household and a two-parent family. Perhaps the hardest task is to give up the relationship with the former spouse. For some reason, even couples who have grown apart and presumably cannot stand each other still have the energy to stay involved with one another by fussing and fighting. In most instances, former spouses realize they cannot count on each other any more for babysitting, sewing on buttons, and changing the oil in the car. While ex-spouses should not expect life as it was, there may be times when they can provide mutual moral support. A supportive ex-spouse will make the road easier for the other parent and also better for the children.

Finally, it is a sad and difficult task for divorcing parents to give up some aspect of the relationship with the child. Normally one parent (the custodial or primary residential parent) must adjust to the notion of giving up total authority and control over the child by encouraging the other parent (the noncustodial or nonprimary residential parent) to have successful parenting times. This means for the PRP to support the NPRP as he or she assumes responsibility for raising of the child during those times. Some parents, of course, must give up living with the child on a day-to-day basis. These parents need to accept the analogy that he or she may be performing with a handicap, but can still play a good game. It is important to understand that if you only see your child once a day, once a week, once a month, or just once a year, you are still the only mom or dad the child will ever have. Every child needs the love and support of both parents.

An important component of acceptance and moving on is forgiveness. In angry divorces, there is plenty of room for forgiveness on both sides. Forgiveness and resentment do not usually coexist. If forgiveness is expressed sincerely and taken seriously—by both the forgiver and the forgiven—it frees up both individuals to move on with their lives.

This idea, that divorced parents and their children need to accept certain inevitable disappointments, will come up at many points in this book. It will be particularly important in: Chapter Seven, "Balancing the Needs of Parents and Children"; Chapter Eight, "Trying To Love Both Parents"; and Chapter Nineteen, "Letting Go and Moving On."

In this book we will be looking at many ideas, suggestions, and solutions. None of these ideas is perfect. Some of these ideas won't work if the other parent is absolutely and totally unreasonable. Children should not be exposed to abusive relationships. In most divorced families, however, both parents have contributed to the dispute. It is fortunate that in most divorced families both ex-spouses have some interest in doing what is best for the children and are looking for solutions.

A basic assumption in this book is the importance for children to have a good relationship with both parents. It is more important for the child to have a good relationship with both parents than it is to have an ideal relationship with one parent and a lousy relationship with the other. The implication of this assumption is that compromise will be required. We compromise at work. We compromise with other adults. It almost seems petty to refuse to compromise with the other most important person in your children's lives. If you don't believe in this assumption, the suggestions and ideas in this book will not make much sense to you.

Chapter Two
Fighting and the Children

In 1986 Robert Butterworth was campaigning for an important office, to become the attorney general of Florida. He was about to be elected. However, he and his ex-wife were also engaged in a custody dispute. On the eve of the election, his ex-wife shot their 16-year-old son four times, called police, and then shot herself.

In 1993 a man in Maryland went to pick up his 4-year-old daughter for visitation. However, he got into an argument with his ex-wife and her boyfriend. The father said that he had a present in his car for the girl. He left the house and went out to the car, but returned with a long box that contained a pump-action shotgun. The man killed his ex-wife; shot the boyfriend as he ran out the door; and then shot himself. When police arrived, they found the little girl standing in the doorway.

In 2001 divorced parents in Tennessee attended a hearing in court regarding their dispute over their son's visitation schedule. The hearing itself was uneventful and the father seemed satisfied with the outcome. In the parking lot of the courthouse, however, the father took a handgun from his car and shot and killed the mother and another woman. The father fled, but later shot himself when he was about to be arrested. The boy was not present, but he lost both his parents on the same day—one by murder and one by suicide.

Parents who are divorcing hurt their children in many ways. What hurts the most is *not* that the parents have left each other, live in separate households, and the children go back and forth. It is *not* the embarrassment that occurs when friends find out the child's parents have split up. It is *not* the decline in the child's standard of living because the family's budget is now spread between two households. What hurts the most is the fighting the children experience. Most of the time the fighting of divorced parents is not as dramatic and brutal as the three stories at the beginning of this chapter, which were taken from newspaper reports from Florida, Maryland, and Tennessee. In most cases the fighting does not erupt into a sudden shootout, but drags on through months and years of painful arguing and bickering.

Remember, divorcing parents involve their children in three methods of fighting: they fight over the children; they fight through the children; and they fight in front of the children. *Fighting over the children* refers to the formal custody dispute conducted in the local courthouse, and also to many informal contests such as the competition to provide the most appreciated birthday present. *Fighting through the children* means one parent's use of the child as a weapon against the other parent. For example, the mother despises her former in-laws, so she withholds visitation because the child "has a fever" on the one weekend they are in town for a visit. Another example is where dad sends the child-support checks through the children and complains how the ex-spouse is taking all his money. A parent puts the child in the middle by making the child call the other parent when scheduling conflicts arise. The meaning of *fighting in front of the children* is more obvious. It usually happens when the NPRP parent arrives to pick up the child for his or her time to spend with the children, and that becomes an opportunity for one or the other parent to address some perceived grievance.

Custody Disputes as Fighting

American customs and legal practices have evolved together to create custody disputes as an expensive, painful, and sometimes tragic ritual. It is sad to watch two concerned and dedicated parents exhausting both their energy and financial resources while fighting over who is the better parent. The gist of most custody disputes is to prove one parent is somehow better (such as, more nurturing, more consistent, more sensible, more decent, more honorable) than the other parent. Disputing parents put much effort into tallying up their respective merits and advantages. Most children, however, do not keep score. They do not notice who is the best provider, who helps with homework, or who is the most fun. Instead they simply love Mom and Dad. They need both parents in their lives so they can see and experience their parents' strengths as well as their weaknesses. Children learn how to deal with important life issues by observing their parents during both good and bad times. This is the only way they can avoid making the same mistakes their parents have made.

The basic custody dispute involves a familiar cast of characters:

- two parents who both feel deeply wronged by each other and whose self-esteem is now derived from the role of parent rather than the role of spouse;
- two attorneys who usually are sincere and well-intentioned and highly partial to the interests of their respective clients;
- a judge, who has heard these same accusations and counter accusations many times;
- the witnesses, various relatives and friends of the parents, who are remarkably one-sided in what they remember about the family;
- sometimes teachers, nannies, and babysitters;
- perhaps a few expert witnesses, such as psychologists and psychiatrists, who try to bring their knowledge and experience to bear on the heavy questions before the court;
- and—almost overlooked as they wait at home or in courthouse hallways—the children.

The expense of this exercise can be enormous in both economic and psychological terms. Consider the financial outlay. The cost of a one-week custody battle in court—including the preparation time billed by two sets of attorneys, the transportation and expenses of various witnesses, and time lost from work—can exceed the annual cost of sending the child to this country's finest private college. We have witnessed custody disputes that cost hundreds of thousands of dollars.

The emotional cost of a custody dispute can also be tremendous. Both parents gear up to identify and attack every vulnerability of the former spouse. This includes exposing in a public trial the most personal and intimate facts—for example, the mother was unfaithful and the father cannot figure out why he married her in the first place; the father worked eighty hours per week while the child was a baby; that one of the parents had a homosexual experience early in life. In other words, both parents gear up to do exactly what the child needs the least, which is to criticize and insult each other and to undermine each other's parenting roles. The emotional cost of the custody dispute is shared among the parents and the children, not to mention the various friends and relatives who have become involved in the process. The battle lines are clearly drawn in these disputes, and the children—in the no-man's-land between the two sides—are caught in the crossfire.

In some states there will be fewer custody disputes because of changes in the laws regarding divorce and children. That is, newer laws

Custody and Visitation Disputes Over Animals

There are occasional reports of custody and visitation disputes involving animals, both dead and alive. We expect that similar cases occur in every community as long as there are litigious people and willing attorneys.

In Montgomery County, Maryland, a divorced couple agreed the former wife would have custody of the couple's dog, while the former husband would have regular visitation. However, the former wife alleged the dog had suffered abuse and neglect while in the care of the former husband, so she withheld additional visitation. By the time the case was heard in court, the Animal Legal Defense Fund filed a brief urging the judge to consider the best interests of the dog. After sorting out the facts and admonishing the human litigants, the judge reinstated the dog's visitation.

In Davidson County, Tennessee, a "reverse custody dispute" occurred over a pet rat at the Juvenile Justice Center. A "reverse custody dispute" is the situation in which the parents are avoiding taking responsibility for a child (or, in this case, a rat). A woman was attempting to turn her son and his pet rat over to the boy's father. The father took the son, but refused to take the rat, court officials said. When neither parent accepted responsibility for the animal, it was abandoned in its cage on the steps of the courthouse. Fortunately, court personnel gave the rat temporary shelter and tried to find a good home for this "charismatic and intelligent pet rodent."

Also in Tennessee, a divorcing couple argued in court over ownership of a frozen turkey. This unusual circumstance arose when both husband and wife received frozen turkeys at Christmas-time from their respective employers. The couple thawed, cooked, and ate one of the turkeys—but they later disagreed as to which one it was. When they subsequently divorced, they both claimed ownership of the remaining frozen turkey. The judge ultimately addressed the dispute over the frozen turkey along with the rest of the property settlement.

require that parents work together to develop, negotiate, and perhaps mediate a parenting plan. In the states that require parenting plans, the parents develop a plan for shared parenting designed specific for their family. Hopefully, this approach will reduce the number of custody disputes and the frequency of relitigation. However, there will always be parents who insist on fighting rather than negotiating—and who will be unable to agree on a parenting plan. In these cases, a judge will have to hear both sides and make the final decisions regarding the child's primary residence and other issues. Perhaps these cases will be called "parenting plan disputes" or "primary residence disputes," rather than custody disputes. This topic is discussed more fully in Chapter Six, "Parenting Education and Parenting Plans."

Attorneys

It is said that there are three types of attorneys:

- Type One: the pushy, powerful, aggressive attorneys known as bombers.
- Type Two: the less aggressive, but basically competent and conscientious attorneys.
- Type Three: the wimpy, ineffectual attorneys.

Each of the three groups contains both male and female attorneys. Numerically, most attorneys who practice family law are Type Twos. There are fewer Type Ones, but they may be better known in the community because they are flamboyant and highly visible. Their philosophy is one of "scorched earth" and "take no prisoners." There are only a few Type Threes because ineffective divorce attorneys are likely to find another line of work.

The fairest and the most sensible legal battles occur when two of the Type Two attorneys litigate against each other. Both of them do a good job. They do what they can to present their clients in a good light. They fight hard, but they fight clean. Also, they usually do not lose sight of the fact that the underlying purpose of these disputes is to determine what is in the best interests of the children. They understand they are building a foundation which will affect this family for decades to come.

It may also seem like a fair fight when each parent has a vigorous, aggressive, Type One attorney, but it is more likely to be a brawl. Type One attorneys may go out of their way to offend or humiliate the other attorney's client; to attack and insult the opposition's witnesses; and to pursue almost any obscure technicality in order to win his or her case. They stir up so much dirt that the children and their interests are lost in a cloud of dust. Sadly, many parents search out these litigators because of their reputations as destroyers. They focus on the courtroom victory instead of the long term best interests of the children.

It is not a fair fight when a more aggressive attorney (a Type One or Type Two) is up against an ineffectual attorney (a Type Three). What happens is that the aggressive attorney browbeats the weak attorney and his client. The more powerful attorney is much more likely to "win," but it may not seem like a just outcome because the victory is based on the lawyer's pushiness rather than on the merits of the case.

Our suggestion to divorcing parents is to work with a Type Two attorney. There are many competent, industrious, and ethical attorneys in every city, so usually it is not hard to locate one who seems right. Since attorneys know their colleagues in the community, you can start your search by checking with a lawyer you many have met at work, at church, in your neighborhood, or in some other legal situation. Tell him or her you want a solid, capable divorce attorney—not a bomber, not a wimp—and ask for recommendations. Interview two or three candidates. Find the one with whom you feel most comfortable as you consider the difficult road ahead. Look for an individual who will help you and your children get on with your lives.

Since divorce is so common, you can ask friends about their experiences with attorneys. Ask specific questions to help in your decision. Did your friend's attorney seem knowledgeable, efficient, smart, and well-organized? Was the attorney effective in reaching a resolution or did the case drag on forever? Did the attorney seem strong and assertive, but not vicious? Did your friend ultimately get what he or she wanted, since that is the purpose of hiring an attorney? Perhaps most importantly, did the attorney take the time and interest in listening to the client's point of view?

Judges

Compared to attorneys, judges appear to come from a more uniform mold. It is true that judges have their own personalities and styles. Some like to dwell on details, while others insist on sticking to the big issues. Some seem talkative and friendly and even humorous, while others are persistently solemn. Some are extremely authoritarian, while others take on a fatherly role toward the divorcing couple and a grandfatherly role toward the children. Despite these superficial differences, it is striking that almost all judges look and act like they are trying to be fair. They seem interested in what every witness brings to the proceedings. What is most important, they are concerned about the children. Although judges accept that it is rarely possible to devise the perfect solution for the children of divorce, they try hard to determine the best alternative of those available.

Sometimes judges do make odd decisions. For instance, one judge could not make up his mind regarding the custody of a 3-year-old girl. After a lengthy hearing, he ruled the parents should have joint custody and the child should alternate between the two households, spending one week at a time at each location. That, in itself, is not a particularly unusual arrangement for a preschool child. The schedule of alternating weeks would not be so bad if a young child had a good relationship with both parents, if the parents lived in the same community, and if the child had the same babysitter in both households or was enrolled in a consistent nursery school.

The problem in this case was that the parents lived in two different communities in two different states, about one hour apart. Since both parents worked, they both had to put the girl in a local day care program. Since they lived so far apart, the parents had to enroll her in two different day care centers and hire two different babysitters. That meant the child had at least six regular caretakers: two parents, two babysitters, and the staff of two day care centers. Unfortunately, these parents could not even agree on the child's hairdo. As the girl passed from one household to the other, both parents would change her physical appearance to suit their own tastes. This little girl had no sense of continuity in her world as she shuttled between her two lives. The judge created a custody arrangement that confused and burdened the child.

Everybody is entitled to his or her own personality traits and idiosyncrasies, including judges. It does create a problem, however, when judges use their position to impose their personal opinions on other people. Occasionally there will be a judge who has very strong beliefs regarding moral issues, child rearing, or sexual behaviors. The judge may feel a particular issue is so important—for example, "young children need a mother more than a father," or "all families should go to church twice a week"—that he does not consider all the pros and cons of the case.

Talk to your attorney about the judge who will be sitting on the bench when your case goes to trial. Keep in mind that many states have laws, guidelines, and protocols that control the scope of the judge's discretion. Your attorney will be able to advise you of the judge's tendencies. Judges are people, too. They have good days and bad days. Some are married, some are divorced, some have children and stepchildren. There are good judges and not-so-good judges, like there are good and not-so-good doctors.

The decision you and your spouse make when you decide to go to court (rather than negotiating a parenting plan) is often short-sighted. Most cases involving child custody disputes last a day or two. You are asking a man or woman who never previously met you or your children to make a decision affecting your family for the next twenty years. Who knows your preferences and your children's needs better, you or the judge? When you ask a judge to make these life-changing decisions, you are giving up your right to choose your own path through the future. Does it make more sense, if possible, for the two most important people in the lives of your children to work together to build a foundation for a long-term relationship? Otherwise, someone else who doesn't know you or your family makes those choices. A judge will do it, but parents should think long and hard before they gamble with their children's future.

Alternatives to Custody Disputes

It is not required that divorcing parents hire extremely expensive attorneys and fight it out in court. There are alternatives. In some divorces the parents simply have a heart-to-heart discussion and decide between themselves how to deal with both financial and custody issues. They ask two attorneys to prepare the agreement up in legal language and present it to a judge. That is all there is to it, with minimal financial and psychological expense.

Parents can sit down together and develop a parenting plan, as described in Chapter Six. These parenting plans are required now in some jurisdictions, but parents in other states can do it on their own and present the plan to the court.

Some individuals make use of divorce mediation. In divorce mediation, a neutral professional, usually an attorney, helps the divorcing couple negotiate out an agreement. For many people, divorce mediation is a great alternative to an adversarial legal dispute. Mediation is discussed in Chapter Eighteen.

Trial's Over, Dispute Continues

The officially recognized manner of fighting over children, the custody dispute, does not last forever. It usually involves the family for several months of preparation time and several days of intense stress, but court proceedings eventually end. In the aftermath of the trial, the failure of the legal system to handle these disputes is most evident. During the custody trial each side destroys the reputation of the other party. Many times it is simply a blood bath with every piece of trash in the other person's life held up for discussion. The lawyers fight their best fight and the judge issues his or her decree. The lawyers go home. The judge retires to his or her chambers. The only people left in this mess of hard feelings are the two ex-spouses, who really hate each other now, and the innocent children. The judge and attorneys wave a magic wand and tell them to go and live happily ever after at their respective homes. It is not surprising that almost forty percent of all initial custody disputes come back to court to relitigate. On the other hand, some divorced parents continue to battle on their own outside of the legal arena.

How bad can it get, this fighting between two individuals who once loved each other? In its most extreme form, the fighting between ex-spouses leads to murder and suicide. That happens often enough that it no longer seems surprising to read in the newspaper about an angry divorced parent who kills his ex-spouse, kills the children, and/or kills himself. Aside from murder and suicide, the fighting between divorced individuals may take many forms. The more fighting, the more the children are victimized. Here are several examples of fighting over the child, through the child, and in front of the child.

- The easiest way to use the child as a weapon is to infuriate the other parent by manipulating the parenting time. For instance, the PRP (primary residential parent) repeatedly says the child can't go anywhere on the weekend because of illness. This ploy may go on for months. For another illustration of this strategy, imagine the frustration in the NPRP (non-primary residential parent) who has driven for five hours to pick up the child for the weekend, only to find the house empty, locked up tight, and nobody in sight. Control of one parent over the other becomes the primary focus. For example, "She has hurt me. Now I will hurt her by keeping the child."

- The NPRP can just as easily misuse his or her parenting time. The child may be returned two hours late because "we ran out of gas." The child may be returned hungry, dirty, or angry, just to annoy the PRP.

- Parents and other relatives may abuse the child through active indoctrination. For example, maternal grandparents instructed a girl to memorize the statements, "My stepmother is a whore. My stepmother is a prostitute and will go to hell." After learning those sentences, she was instructed to recite them when she stayed with her father and stepmother. Most children love their parents, stepparents, and grandparents. When family members undermine these relationships, the children will suffer for a lifetime.

   •   Some parents fight each other by making spurious allegations of sexual abuse. They may indoctrinate the child or coerce the child to make statements describing the abuse. Of course, actual sexual abuse can be damaging both physically and psychologically. It is also damaging to put the child in the position of making false allegations.

   •   An interesting form of fighting through the child occurs when each parent claims to be doing what is absolutely best for the child. Sometimes it takes the form of religious instruction. For example, one parent may have the child enrolled in Sunday school at the Catholic parish church. The other parent, however, takes the child to Jewish services every other weekend and has him studying Hebrew. If the child ends up confused and resentful, who is to blame? Each parent has the legal right to raise the child in his or her own religion, but does it really make sense to insist on ruthlessly exercising that right? Once again, control becomes the issue instead of raising a well adjusted child.

   •   Another issue that puts the child in the middle of parental conflict is the child's appearance. Both parents may have strong opinions about what clothing the child should wear and what kind of haircut he should have. Imagine how much anger is aroused when the mother wants her son to have long hair and the father delivers the boy with a crew cut after his parenting time.

   •   Many parents use financial issues as a rationalization for fighting in a way that involves the children. Perhaps the most common is the PRP who withholds parenting time because the NPRP failed to pay child support. In many states, this clearly violates the law. Likewise, an affluent NPRP may withhold money unless he gets his way in certain areas. Child support cannot provide for all the needs of the child. Flexibility and parental involvement is the key.

   •   Even after the custody dispute is over, divorced parents may continue to fight it out in court. For example, a PRP who is passive-aggressive may force the NPRP to file a law suit every time he wants something that should have been accomplished through routine nego-

Custody Disputes of the Rich and Famous

Several famous custody disputes came out of Hollywood. *Kramer vs. Kramer* was a popular movie in 1979 featuring Dustin Hoffman and Meryl Streep. When the mother in the movie left the home and dropped out of sight, the father had to rely on his own devices to raise their son, Billy Kramer. The father took Billy to school, cooked his meals, and tried to hold down a job. After being absent for 18 months, the mother came to realize she wanted to be a parent again. She wanted custody of Billy. The parents went to court to resolve the legal dispute of *Kramer vs. Kramer*. If you missed the movie, you can find out what happened by placing a special order at your local video store.

In 1993 Woody Allen and Mia Farrow waged a bitter and turbulent battle over their three children, Moses, Dylan, and Satchel. The media focused on Mr. Allen's romantic relationship with Ms. Farrow's older (adopted) child, Soon-Yi Previn, which most people found extremely inappropriate. There were accusations that Mr. Allen had sexually abused his adoptive daughter, Dylan. In the end, the judge reportedly said Mr. Allen was an inadequate and irresponsible parent. It was painful for the average person to read about this custody trial in the daily papers, so it must have been a nightmare for the participants. It certainly illustrates how children are the victims when their parents fight each other.

In June 1994, Nicole Brown Simpson and Ronald Goldman were brutally killed. At the time, Nicole Simpson and O.J. Simpson were separated. Their children, Sydney (age 8 at the time) and Justin (age 5), were living with their mother. O.J. Simpson was charged with murder and while he awaited trial and during his trial, the children were in the custody of their maternal grandparents. When Simpson was acquitted of the two murders in 1995, he regained custody of Sydney and Justin from the grandparents. Even after a civil trial—under a lower standard of proof—found Simpson responsible for the deaths of Nicole Simpson and Ronald Goldman, the children continued to live with their father. According to news reports, Simpson and the maternal grandparents ultimately reached an agreement—in which Simpson had physical custody of Sydney and Justin, while the grandparents retained legal guardianship of the children.

tiation. On the other hand, much time and huge sums of money may be
expended in trying to impose unreasonable demands on one's former
spouse.

•   Parental fighting may seem almost bizarre to outside observers. Consider the woman on *Court TV* who presented her case, which
was based on the father's having said bad things about her to their child.
After the trial the woman was interviewed for the television audience
and she repeated how horrible the father had been to badmouth her to
the child, and she insisted she had never said a bad thing about the
father. There she was on national television criticizing the father's
parenting abilities!

In these scenarios the child is caught in the middle, which may
cause her to have psychological problems or may lead to the development of innovative coping skills. For example, the child who is caught
between two fighting parents may discover how to be diplomatic every
day in every way. She finds that it works best to agree with the mother
when she is with her and to agree with the father when she is with him.
On the other hand, in order to avoid being caught in the middle, some
children gravitate to being completely allied with one parent or the other.
In other words, they become overly attached and identified with one
parent (usually the PRP) and alienated from the other parent (usually
the NPRP). This phenomenon is discussed in chapter eight, "Trying to
Love Both Parents."

Solutions

The fighting and consequent emotional trauma to the children of
divorce are neither desirable nor necessary. There are many possible
solutions.

•   Both parents should understand the children will be better off if
they continue to have a good relationship with both the mother and the
father. Both parents need to accept and work toward that goal. This is
easier said than done, but many divorcing parents are able to set aside
their grievances and work together on behalf of the children. For example, a 12-year-old boy was having both academic and behavioral problems and was suspended from school several times. The youngster was
referred for a psychological evaluation and both parents readily participated in the testing and in the counseling, although they had been di-

vorced for several years. The counselor helped the parents communicate with each other as well as with their son.

•   Parenting time is usually a happier occasion if it operates like clockwork—that is, the schedule is reliable and predictable, especially during the first year or so after the divorce. The best bet is to set up a schedule months ahead of time and then stick to it. The schedule should be detailed, concrete, and refer to specific days and specific times. The parenting time of both the mother and father should start on time and end on time. This kind of rigid schedule is helpful during the first year of the divorce because it means there is one less issue to discuss and argue about. After everyone has become more comfortable with their new roles, it is possible to be more flexible with the parenting-time schedule.

•   It seems odd that a minor illness, such as a runny nose or a low fever, should prevent parenting time from occurring. It seems to us that the NPRP should be encouraged to take care of the child both in sickness and in health. By doing this, the child will be able to rely on two parents to care for him when he faces difficult times.

•   It should be obvious that parents, grandparents, and other interested parties should not try to influence and mentally intimidate the children. Even though children are a captive audience, parents should forego the temptation to engage in any form of indoctrination or brainwashing. Fortunately, some children are able to protect themselves from indoctrination. With appropriate discussion and support, such children are able to ignore these malicious activities. A child may learn to say, "Mommy, I really don't want to talk about Daddy any more."

•   If a mother thinks that the father may have abused the child, what should she do? Before running off to the Rape Crisis Center, consider what you would have done if you were still married. You probably would have sat down and directly asked the other parent what had happened. One time a little girl told her mother, the PRP, that her daddy had hurt her peepee during the weekend visitation. The mother looked and, sure enough, the girl's genital area was red. The mother called protective services and an investigation was undertaken. The child was interviewed by a social worker and a police officer. Eventually the father was contacted and interviewed. He said that over the weekend he had noticed his daughter had a diaper rash. He consulted the pediatrician, who recommended an ointment. He thought the ointment may have hurt the child a little when he put it on her. The pediatrician confirmed this account. It would have saved everybody a lot of trouble if the worried mother had simply checked with the father in the first place and asked him what happened over the weekend.

•   Parents should try to communicate and agree as much as possible—such as whether the child is going to take ballet or tap-dancing this year; whether the child's attention-deficit problem is severe enough to consider medication; whether the youngster is allowed to see PG-13 movies. The actual nature of the communication depends on the amount of trust and respect between the parents. If there is still a good deal of anger or friction, it will work better to use regular, written communication, perhaps every couple of weeks. But send the notes through the mail or e-mail, not hand-delivered by the child.

•   If the parents cannot agree on some items, they should consider dividing up the decisions and allowing each parent to take responsibility for specific issues. For example: the mother might be totally in charge of the child's birthday party this year; the father will be totally in charge of the science fair project; or vice versa. The point is that it does not matter so much which parent is going to do which aspect of parenting, but to agree on a division of labor and then stick to it.

•   Another way to avoid conflict is for each parent to make plans and arrangements in a way that does not involve the other parent. A NPRP might work with the child in developing a particular interest or hobby (dinosaurs, cooking, rock collecting, whatever) in a way that does not need to involve the PRP.

•   A way to act independently and avoid conflict is for the NPRP to pay for some expenses directly, without going through the PRP. If the child is in a private school, for instance, the NPRP can pay her part of the tuition directly to the school rather than through the PRP.

•   Some of these suggestions seem contradictory. That's correct! Sometimes it is better to discuss, negotiate, and agree. Other times it is better for divorced parents to divide the tasks of child-rearing and work independently. Parents needs to figure out which approach to use in different circumstances. In all cases, however, the underlying motivation is for both parents to be involved and to protect the child from conflict. It is critical for parents to choose a course that will provide the best environment for the child to flourish.

•   At times divorced parents are not able to work out these issues on their own. They may need professional assistance such as: educational programs for divorced parents; counseling by a mental health professional; or divorce mediation. These topics are discussed in Chapter Seventeen "Mental Health Professionals," and in Chapter Eighteen "Divorce Mediation and Divorce Counseling."

•   Finally, parents might be able to reduce arguing by being flexible and creative in designing the residential arrangements and other details of the parenting plan. They might consider a schedule in which the children live in one house during the week every week and in the other house every weekend. If there are several children, they might consider allowing some of the children to live primarily with one parent and some of the children to live primarily with the other parent. The reason these unusual arrangements reduce the strife is because they tend to empower both parents equally. That is, they help both parents feel like full-time, contributing parents and the result is there is less arguing about each other's territory. "Uncommon Parenting Arrangements" are discussed in Chapter Five.

The message of this chapter is simple enough. Children of divorce can usually handle the reality that Mom and Dad are not going to be living together anymore. They can usually handle the confusion and inconvenience of having a somewhat complicated schedule during the course of the week or the month. They can usually handle the knowledge that their parents disagree at times. What they cannot handle easily is the incessant arguing and intense fighting. There are many ways for thoughtful parents to reduce the amount of conflict their children experience.

Chapter Three
Divorce Trials and Tribulations

Although they were never married, Ana and William had a custody dispute over their 2-year-old son, which eventually reached the Supreme Court of California.

Initially, when Ana told William that she was pregnant with his child, William refused to believe her. After the child was born, William continued to deny paternity and withheld child support. Ana cared for the child by taking two jobs and relied on the help of friends, family, and daycare facilities. Ana brought a paternity suit against William in order to obtain child support. Blood tests established that William was the child's father and the court ordered William to pay $200 a month to Ana. When William visited his son for the first time, a reconciliation began and William moved in with Ana and their son in an attempt to live together as a family. The attempt failed, and William moved out.

When William asked for visitation with his son, Ana refused and sought exclusive custody. William also sought exclusive custody of the child. In fact, the child's custody had not previously been established by any court, so the judge proceeded to assign custody based on an assessment of the best interests of the child. Applying the "best interests" test, the court awarded custody to William. The court based its decision on these considerations: (1) William was financially better off. He had greater job stability and owned his own home. (2) William had remarried. The court thought William and the stepmother could provide constant care for the child without resorting to other caretakers.

This case was appealed to the Supreme Court of California. The Supreme Court said the lower court's decision referring to William's better economic advantage was not a permissible basis for a custody award. The Court stated, "If in fact the custodial parent's income is insufficient to provide a proper care for the child, the remedy is to award child support, not to take away custody." The lower court referred to how the child's mother, Ana, worked and had to place the child in daycare, while William's new wife could care for the child in their home. The Supreme

Court of California stated, "The courts must not presume a working mother is a less satisfactory parent or less fully committed to the care of the child, when over 50 percent of mothers and almost 80 percent of divorced mothers work." The Supreme Court of California thought a custody determination should be based upon a true assessment of the emotional bonds between the parent and child. It must also reflect a factual determination of how best to provide continuity of attention, nurturing, and care. The Supreme Court reversed the lower court's ruling and awarded the mother, Ana, custody of her child.

This case (*Burchard vs. Garay,* 42 Cal.3d 531) occurred in 1986 in California, but it could have occurred in any state at any time during the last century. The purpose of citing this example is not to elucidate the exact meaning of the "best interests" rule in court. Instead, our purpose is simpler—to show how heart-wrenching it is to fight out these issues in court. It can be a nightmare for the mother, the father, and especially the child.

No one wins a contested divorce trial. Sadly, those who suffer most are the children of the broken marriage. Usually it works out best for divorcing parents to develop a reasonable parenting plan on their own or perhaps with the assistance of a mediator and their attorneys. In reality, however, some cases must be resolved with the assistance of a judge. The purpose of this chapter is to discuss the proper procedure for litigating these difficult cases and the best way to present evidence in a trial over custody or parenting time.

In today's trials involving custody or the child's residential arrangements, the parties and their respective counsel commit great error by adopting the strategy that the only way to succeed is to prove the other party is unfit to be the primary residential parent. This is almost an impossible task and involves a great deal of expense, both financially and emotionally. It takes more time and effort to develop an all-out assault on the character of the person to whom you previously professed your undying love than it does to concentrate on the best interests of the child.

We suggest an alternative strategy. In the event a trial is the only solution to resolve custody issues, it is critical for counsel and their clients to pursue a course toward substantiating what is in the best interests of the child instead of pursuing what is in the best interests of the parent. The notion that custody disputes should be decided on the basis of the best interests of the child is old news. In fact, this idea was

---

Important Case: *Finlay vs. Finlay* (240 N.Y. 429)

Mr. A. Lugar Finlay, a resident of Missouri, brought an action against his wife, Dorothea Finlay, a resident of New York, for a judgment regulating the custody of their infant children. Mr. and Mrs. Finlay formerly had their home together in Westchester County, New York. In early 1923, Dorothea took the children with her and refused to live with her husband. Following the abandonment, Lugar moved to Missouri. The children were with the mother in New York, and she refused to give them up. Lugar sought a judgment that would enable him to share with Dorothea the custody of the children.

This dispute reached the Court of Appeals of New York, the highest court in the state. The opinion was written by a famous jurist, Justice Benjamin Cardozo, in 1925. Justice Cardozo explained how the trier-of-fact, the chancellor, should address cases like this: "He acts as parens patriae to do what is best for the interest of the child. He is to put himself in the position of a wise, affectionate and careful parent," and make provisions for the child accordingly.

---

stated clearly for the first time in a trial that took place in 1925. That case, *Finlay vs. Finlay* (240 N.Y. 429), is summarized in the box on this page.

Of course, there has been a continuing debate as to exactly what constitutes the best interests of the child. A fairly simple way to address the issue was to adopt "the tender years presumption," which meant young children were almost always put in the custody of their mothers. The assumption was that mothers were by nature physically and emotionally better suited to take care of young children than were fathers. In the United States, the origin of the tender years presumption is attributed to the 1830 Maryland decision of *Helms vs. Franciscus* (2 Bland 544) stating it would violate the laws of nature to "snatch" an infant from the care of its mother. This idea was the basis for most court decisions until the 1980s, when important cases weakened or even removed the tender years presumption.

In the landmark case, *Ex parte Christopher Devine* (398 So.2d 686), the Supreme Court of Alabama said the tender years presumption violated the Fourteenth Amendment of the United States Constitution. The Fourteenth Amendment says, in part: "No state shall make or en-

---

Important Case: *Ex parte Christopher Devine* (398 So.2d 686)

Christopher Devine and Alice Devine were married in 1966. Two sons were born during their marriage. When the couple separated in 1979, the court awarded custody of both children, ages 4 and 7, to Alice. In Alabama law at that time, a presumption existed that when dealing with children of tender years, the natural mother was presumed, in absence of evidence to the contrary, to be the proper person to be vested with custody of such children. In this case, it was clear either the mother or the father would be a fit and proper person to be vested with the care, custody, and control of the parties' minor children.

In 1981 this dispute reached the Supreme Court of Alabama where the father stated the tender years presumption was unconstitutional because it violated his Fourteenth Amendment rights. The Supreme Court of Alabama concluded, "The tender years presumption represents an unconstitutional gender-based classification which discriminates between fathers and mothers in child custody proceedings solely on the basis of sex." By requiring fathers to carry the difficult burden of affirmatively proving the unfitness of the mother, the presumption may have had the effect of depriving some loving fathers of the custody of their children, while enabling some alienated mothers to arbitrarily obtain temporary custody.

force any law which shall abridge the privileges or immunities of citizens of the United States; nor shall any state deprive any person of life, liberty, or property, without due process of law; nor deny to any person within its jurisdiction the equal protection of the laws." In other words, the Court thought the tender years presumption did not give equal protection to mothers and fathers. The case of *Devine* is summarized in the box on this page.

For a long time, fathers were unable to win custody of their children unless they were able to show the mother was unfit. Usually, a person would have to have major problems to be considered an unfit parent for his or her child. Since the courts decided in the 1980s that mothers and fathers would have a level playing field, they needed to articulate a new standard or set of principles on which to assign custody in contested cases. For example, the judge in a Tennessee case, *Bah vs. Bah*

Important Case: *Bah vs. Bah* (668 S.W.2d 663)

In this case, Thierno Abubaker Bah and Sarah Francis Oden Bah sought a divorce and there was a dispute regarding the custody of the couple's 2½-year-old son. The trial court awarded the father custody of the child based on the following findings of fact: Sarah admitted she committed adultery; both parties initially participated in the rearing of the child and both parties exhibited parenting skills; Sarah behaved in a manner that jeopardized the welfare of the child; and Sarah behaved in an immature and irresponsible manner, exhibited emotional instability, and disrupted the life of the child for insignificant reasons. The court found "the husband was the most stable and emotionally mature parent at the time." In awarding custody to the father, the court stated the "tender years doctrine" was only one factor to be considered in the overall determination of what was in the best interests of the child.

In 1983, this case reached the Court of Appeals of Tennessee, which affirmed the judgment of the trial court. The Court of Appeals adopted what it considered a common sense approach to custody, that is, the doctrine of "comparative fitness." The Court of Appeals restated the paramount concern in child custody cases is the welfare and best interests of the child.

(668 S.W.2d 663), made use of the concept of "comparative fitness" rather than the tender years pre-sumption. The case of *Bah vs. Bah* is summarized in the box on this page.

Many states now provide a roadmap toward the goal of basing custody decisions on the best interests of the child. In other words, rather than letting judges rely on a series of important court cases, the state legislatures passed laws that listed and defined the criteria for judges to use in deciding these cases. In Tennessee, for instance, the law lists a number of elements judges must consider in making these life-changing determinations (Tennessee Code § 36-6-404). It is appropriate for counsel to center his or her presentation on these issues.

It is important to note this list of significant factors is not all-inclusive and may vary from jurisdiction to jurisdiction. For purposes of this discussion the Tennessee Code (**text in bold, below**) will be used to provide direction as to how a case should proceed. These are the factors a judge should consider in deciding which parent will be the primary residential parent.

The first criterion listed in the Tennessee Code is: **The parent's ability to instruct, inspire, and encourage the child to prepare for a life of service, and to compete successfully in the society which the child faces as an adult.** Evidence to prove this element may be presented regarding the proposed living environment and atmosphere of the home as well as the various elements of support involving the child. The parent who desires to be designated the primary residential parent should demonstrate his or her plan to accomplish this goal of preparing the child for the future. This could include evidence of previous accomplishments in extracurricular activities, homework schedules, and school schedules. While future plans for the child are important, proof of past activities are normally relevant.

The next factor is: **The relative strength, nature, and stability of a child's relationship with each parent, including whether a parent has taken greater responsibility for performing parenting responsibilities relating to the daily needs of the child.** It is important to develop proof that the parent in question has, in fact, performed many of the parenting responsibilities in the past, such as taking the child to the doctor, attending parent/teacher conferences, and participating in other extracurricular activities. It may be appropriate to have testimony from medical or mental health professionals to present evidence of the child's reliance upon a particular parent. Many attorneys believe the best way to prove this element is to call the child as a witness, although we believe every effort should be made to avoid having the child testify in court. Instead, parents should be dedicated to proving the strength of their relationship with the child through: their own testimony; the testimony of friends, relatives, and teachers; and any medical and psychological proof.

It is easy to see why judges (in deciding individual cases) and legislators (in making state laws) should consider it very important as to which parent was more involved in taking care of the day-to-day needs of the child. Basically, the parent who previously was the primary caretaker is likely to be the more motivated and dedicated parent in the future. A landmark case in West Virginia spelled out the various factors the court should address in determining which parent was the primary caretaker. The case of *Garska vs. McCoy* (278 S.E.2d 357) is summarized in the box on page 34.

The next criterion is: **The willingness and ability of each of the**

Important Case: *Garska vs. McCoy* (278 S.E.2d 357)

Michael Garska and Gwendolyn McCoy were the unwed parents of Jonathan McCoy, who was born in 1978. During the pregnancy and after the birth of Jonathan, the father provided minimal support to the mother.

Jonathan had chronic respiratory infections that required hospitalizations. Ms. McCoy arranged for her grandparents to adopt Jonathan so the child's medical care would be paid by the United Mine Worker's insurance. However, Mr. Garska, upon hearing the plan of adoption, visited the child for the first time and began paying $15 a week in child support. When Mr. Garska filed a petition to gain custody of his son, the circuit court awarded him custody because "he was the child's natural father, was more intelligent and better educated than the mother, was better able to provide financial support and could provide a better social environment."

In 1981, this case reached the Supreme Court of Appeals of West Virginia, which reversed the findings of the previous court and awarded custody to the mother. The Supreme Court of Appeals found that in a custody dispute involving children of tender years, the Circuit Court must determine which parent is the primary caretaker and ensure that parent is fit. There are criteria the court must consider in its determination: (1) preparing and planning of meals; (2) bathing, grooming, and dressing; (3) purchasing, cleaning, and care of clothes; (4) medical care, including nursing and trips to physicians; (5) arranging for social interaction among peers after school, i.e., transporting to friends' houses or, for example, to girl or boy scout meetings; (6) arranging alternative care, i.e., babysitting, day-care, etc.; (7) putting child to bed at night, attending to child in middle of the night, waking child in the morning; (8) disciplining, i.e., teaching general manners and toilet training; (9) educating, i.e., religious, cultural, social, etc.; and (10) teaching elementary skills, i.e., reading, writing, and arithmetic.

In applying these criteria, the court found the mother was the primary caretaker and the father's alleged superior position with regard to economics and education "pales in comparison to love, affection, concern, tolerance and the willingness to sacrifice." The court found the mother's consent to adoption did not reflect intent to abandon the child, but rather "solicitous concern for his welfare."

**parents to facilitate and encourage a close and continuing par-
ent-child relationship between the child and the other parent,
consistent with the best interests of the child.** This factor can simply be known as the "get-along-with-each-other" provision. The parent
needs to introduce proof of how he or she worked in the past to facilitate
a working parental relationship with the ex-spouse in spite of their differences and inability to live together as husband and wife. A track record
of willingness to cooperate for the well being of the child is essential. It
is appropriate to propose a parenting-time schedule as evidence of the
parent's willingness to promote a positive relationship with the other
parent. In fact, this schedule should be drawn in such a way that, if the
proposing party is not successful in his or her request for designation,
the party would be willing to live with his or her proposed agreement as
the non-primary residential parent.

Next: **Willful refusal to attend a court-ordered parent education seminar may be considered by the court as evidence of a
parent's lack of good faith in these proceedings.** In many states,
there are laws requiring divorcing parents to attend parent-education
seminars. In addition, it is wise to present evidence of additional parenting
classes in which the mother or father participated. Normally, failure to
attend a parent-education seminar cannot be used as a judicial basis to
deny a divorce. However, parents can be found in contempt and possibly
sentenced to jail for failure to attend these important classes. It is hard
to imagine a parent who is truly interested in the long-term well-being
of their children but is not willing to spend four hours learning about
the effects of divorce on those same children.

The next element to consider: **The disposition of each parent to
provide the child with food, clothing, medical care, education
and other necessary care.** The plan for the child's education is a critical element for judges in making their decisions. To be successful in
proving a commitment to education, it would be appropriate to put forth
proof as to where the child will be attending school. If possible, examples
of curricula and testimony from school officials as to how the child will
be incorporated into the academic environment should be included in
this proof. In the event of a change of schools, it may be important to
have a psychologist or psychiatrist testify as to the willingness or ability
of the child to adjust to the new environment. Regarding medical care,
knowledge of health problems and challenges should be exhibited in the
parent's testimony. Also, planning for future medical needs should be
part of the proof submitted to the trier of fact. The court will also take

into account the living arrangements of the parties, and presentations should be made regarding housing plans, access to playgrounds, home activities, and the schedule of regular events. Proof should be presented with regard to current situations and not just speculation about what might happen in the future.

A court will further consider: **The degree to which a parent has been the primary caregiver, defined as the parent who has taken the greater responsibility for performing parental responsibilities.** In assessing each parent's role in providing for the day-to-day care of the child, the parent's previous track record is important but not the only element considered. Children need stability and a positive living arrangement is very important, so many courts look to the past to see who has taken the greater responsibility for performing parental duties for the child. If you are the parent who has been the past primary care giver, it is critical to put forth proof to substantiate this claim. If you are not, then proof needs to be introduced as to how you intend to accept this new responsibility.

Another criterion is: **The love, affection, and emotional ties existing between each parent and the child.** Obviously, the parent can testify as to his or her love and affection for the child, but the parent may also need testimony by a mental health expert regarding the child's emotional ties to family members. This can be accomplished through psychological testing and other alternatives, which are important in a judge's decision regarding the long-term best interests of the child.

Tennessee also considers: **The emotional needs and developmental level of the child.** Proof about social performance at school, emotional development, and goals for the child should be introduced. Evidence as to how the child achieved these accomplishments in the past should be presented.

The court will also consider: **The character and physical and emotional fitness of each parent as it relates to each parent's ability to parent or the welfare of the child.** In support of this element, it may be important to compare and contrast the physical and emotional fitness as well as the moral character of each party. To this end, it is more effective to demonstrate why one person is the better parent than to expend energy and effort toward demeaning the other parent. It is similar to applying for a job. During a job interview, it is not best to take the time to run down the other candidates, but instead to promote oneself in the best light. It has also been suggested this would be a better course of action if one were truly interested in the long-term best interests of the child. However, this does not mean that if one parent has a history of negative behavior and failures in caring for the child it should not be disclosed to the court. Indeed, this evidence is important, but many times it is presented to the exclusion of long-range plans for the development of the child.

The next element the court will deliberate is: **The child's interaction and interrelationships with siblings and with significant adults, as well as the child's involvement with the child's physical surroundings, school, or other significant activities.** For this, proof needs to focus on third-party support such as the child's relationships with grandparents, uncles, aunts, and siblings. Information regarding church and neighborhood support systems should also be submitted. Most people agree children need to be raised in nurturing, secure environments. Third-party support, especially where parents are not living together, is critical not only for the well being of the parent but also for the child. In the event a move is suggested, substantial evidence should focus on how the daily life, interactions, and important relationships will be maintained.

One area to which the court normally gives great weight to is: **The importance of continuity in the child's life and the length of time the child has lived in a stable, satisfactory environment.** Basically, courts have adopted the philosophy that children are happiest when they can remain in the environment to which they have been accustomed during their formative years. Due to the financial devastation of divorce, this is not always possible. This becomes quite difficult when one party wants to maintain the same household or live in the same neighborhood while the other party desires to move from the area. In order to maintain a meaningful relationship with both parents, the mother and father must strive to remain in close proximity to each other. However, in today's mobile society, this is not always possible and may not be feasible. See Chapter Twelve, "Moving Near and Far."

The court should consider: **Evidence of physical or emotional abuse to the child, to the other parent or to any other person.** This is one area for which proof is critical to demonstrate that one spouse has abused the other parent, the child, or other individuals. Of course, this element relates back to the character of the parties. In divorce cases, proof regarding abuse is quite variable. In some instances, it is obvious—based on medical records, testimony, and information from child protection agencies—that spousal abuse or child abuse occurred in the family. However, false allegations of abuse also sometimes occur in the context of high conflict divorces. It may take considerable effort on the part of investigators, medical personnel, mental health evaluators, and the court itself to determine what actually occurred.

The court should also contemplate: **The character and behavior of any other person who resides in or frequents the home of a parent and such person's interactions with the child.** Individuals such as new partners, stepchildren, and other family members will be included in this element. It is not recommended new adult relationships be introduced into a family going through a separation or divorce. Life is challenging enough during this difficult time—with financial repercussions, relocation, and the emotional trauma of divorce—without adding the challenges of a new relationship. This changing environment will also have an emotional impact on the children. In court, evidence should be submitted regarding the presence of other people who have been introduced to the minor child. There should be evidence of the character and emotional stability of these third parties and how the child has interacted with them in the past. Once again, psychological proof may be introduced to show how this new relationship has been or might be positive or negative to the child.

In many states, the court considers the following: **The reasonable preference of a child if 12 years of age or older. The court may hear the preference of a younger child upon request. The preference of older children should normally be given greater weight than those of younger children.** This is a very important element not only for the parent but also for the child. In many states there is no age limit in presenting testimony regarding a child's preference. Also, parents and their respective counsel should think long and hard before subjecting a child to this type of pressure, even if it takes place in the judge's chambers and not in the courtroom. Judges give no more weight to this element than they do the others. Allowing the child to testify sets up further conflict because the child will assume he or she is the decision maker about the primary residence and the parenting schedule. Many times the child threatens to relocate every time he does not get his way or one parent is more of a disciplinarian than the other parent. Sadly, to allow children to testify as to their preference toward one parent or another puts them in an awkward position, can be harmful to them, and is not in their long-term best interests.

The court also looks at: **Each parent's employment schedule, and the court may make accommodations consistent with those**

schedules. The court will try to determine how each parent's work schedule relates to the best interests of the child. In the event childcare is necessary, it is important to put forth proof as to where the child will be staying during the day and with whom. Once again, it is better to have a plan in place and not merely a promise to modify a work schedule. Witnesses such as childcare providers are important because the court is quite interested in the day-to-day care of the child.

Our current court system does little to develop a foundation for a long-term working relationship between ex-spouses, and a contested divorce trial makes that goal even more elusive. It is important, if possible, for parents to avoid these bitter battles. Instead, the mother and father should work toward providing an environment where the focus is simply on the well-being of the children of divorce.

Chapter Four
Common Parenting Arrangements

Giacomo Puccini's famous opera, Madame Butterfly, *is extremely sentimental and sad. The story line of the opera was a love story and a custody dispute at a time when it was assumed the father had an absolute right to have custody of his child.*

The opera was set in Nagasaki, Japan, around 1900. An officer in the United States Navy, Lieutenant B. F. Pinkerton, arrived at the port city of Nagasaki and married a Japanese Geisha, "Butterfly." They conceived a son, whose name was Sorrow. Lieutenant Pinkerton promptly sailed back to the United States and left his wife to be the primary—in fact, the exclusive—caretaker of their son. Butterfly raised the child in an adoring manner and waited patiently for the father's return to the family.

After three years Lieutenant Pinkerton did return. But in the meantime he had married an American woman named Kate, and he had the nerve to bring her with him when he returned to Japan! It soon became clear that Lieutenant Pinkerton and his new wife had come to Nagasaki simply to pick up the child and take him away. Butterfly was, of course, devastated. In one short scene she realized she no longer had a husband, his new wife was standing in her living room, and she was about to lose her cherished son.

Butterfly told Pinkerton and Kate to leave her alone with Sorrow for a few minutes, and then they could come and take the child. In the last moments of the opera, Butterfly sat Sorrow down, blindfolded him, and put a little American flag in his hands. Then she killed herself. At that moment, Lieutenant Pinkerton returned to see Butterfly's death and take the child whom he had demanded.

A Short History of Child Custody

In the nineteenth century divorce was infrequent and when it did occur it was usually assumed the father would have custody of the children. The husband had control over the marital property and that included the children. In *Madame Butterfly,* it was simply taken for granted that the father had the right to possess the little boy, even though he had not laid eyes on Trouble for three years.

In the twentieth century divorce became more common and courts held that children should generally be raised by their mothers. The notion seemed to be: husbands/fathers were more likely to be working and were not available to raise the children; wives/mothers were more likely to be homemakers and were also more nurturing. This was called the "tender years doctrine," which was the premise that mothers were considered better qualified to raise children than fathers.

In the latter part of the twentieth century women's liberation occurred (so mothers were more likely to have careers and be working full time) and also men's liberation (so fathers were more likely to insist on being considered full-fledged nurturing parents). The end result was that most courts came to believe the mother and father should have an equal opportunity to be the custodial parent. However, many people still think very young children, such as infants, are more appropriately raised by their mothers.

In the twenty-first century, who knows what will become of the nuclear family unit and what will be considered normal parenting arrangements? The frequency of divorce will probably continue to increase. Hopefully, parents and society in general will find ways to nurture the many children of divorced parents.

The Traditional Custodial Parent

The most common arrangement in our country is for one of the divorcing parents to become the permanent custodial parent and for the other to be the noncustodial parent. The terminology—"custodial" and "noncustodial" parent—depends on the state where the divorce occurs. The majority of states still have laws using these terms, so most of this chapter pertains directly to those jurisdictions. The legislators of some states have made an effort to make new laws in which the terms "custodial" and "noncustodial" are not used at all. The problem has been that noncustodial parents felt disempowered— because the word "noncustodial" implies the parent is not a full parent and because noncustodial parents have experienced limited rights in some states. The way to avoid using these words is to develop a parenting plan, which specifies the child's schedule and defines the rights and responsibilities of both parents without ever indicating one parent has

Books Regarding Child Custody

There are several books for parents who want further information about custodial arrangements and how they come about, as well as parenting after divorce has occurred.

Here are two classic books regarding divorce and children, which were originally published in the 1980s. *Mom's House, Dad's House: A Complete Guide for Parents Who are Separated, Divorced, or Living Apart,* by Isolina Ricci (Fireside, 1997, revised edition) was one of the first books to emphasize joint custody and shared parenting.

Also, *Crazy Time: Surviving Divorce & Building a New Life,* by Abigail Trafford (Harper Paperbacks, 1992, revised edition) focuses on how to get through the divorce itself. Trafford, a divorce lawyer, explains and normalizes the strong feelings that divorcing men and women experience.

Uncoupling: Turning Points in Intimate Relationships, by Diane Vaughn (Vintage, 1990) addresses how to let go of your former partner and move on with you life. It is based on sociological and psychological research.

Parent vs. Parent: How You and Your Child Can Survive the Custody Battle, by Stephen Herman (Pantheon Books, 1990) focuses on the custody dispute and its resolution. The author, a child and adolescent psychiatrist, advises parents on how to minimize the trauma their children experience.

The Good Divorce, by Constance R. Ahrons (Harper Paperbacks, 1998) introduced the term, "binuclear families," Ahrons, who has conducted research on divorced families, says that parents who approach divorce in a healthy manner can end up stronger, not damaged.

How to Help Your Child Overcome Your Divorce: A Support Guide for Families, by Elissa P. Benedek and Catherine F. Brown (Newmarket Press, 2001) instructs parents on how to help their children adjust to separation and divorce. The senior author, Elissa P. Benedek, is a former president of the American Psychiatric Association.

What About the Kids? Raising Your Children Before, During, and After Divorce, by Judith S. Wallerstein and Sandra Blakeslee (Hyperion, 2003) is based on decades of research at The Center for the Family in Transition in California. The authors offer advice for parents going through divorce and also dealing with its aftermath.

Divorce for Dummies, by John Ventura and Mary Reed (For Dummies, 2005, second edition) gives general information regarding divorce, including financial and legal tips.

custody and the other does not. See Chapter Six for how to develop a parenting plan.

In jurisdictions that still have custodial and noncustodial parents, the children of course live primarily with the custodial parent. The children almost always have regular visitation with the noncustodial parent. The basic reasoning for this arrangement is that it is important for children to feel they have a definite, permanent home; to have consistent parenting by the same individual; and to develop roots by living in the same community among the same close friends and relatives. It is also important for the children to have a fulfilling, satisfying relationship with the noncustodial parent, so visitation should be endorsed, encouraged, and facilitated by the custodial parent.

In this common, routine custody arrangement the custodial parent has the responsibility and the authority to make the major decisions regarding the child. That would include decisions such as school placement, medical care, and whether the child should be in counseling for an emotional problem. In practice, the custodial parent usually controls many details of the child's life, such as who his friends are, what his hobbies might be, and how much homework he does every night.

In many divorced families the custodial and the noncustodial parents raise the children in a reasonably harmonious manner and the children thrive. The children find ways to relate to both parents, to identify with both parents, and to learn from both parents. This arrangement works when the parents put effort into communicating with each other regarding the children, even though they may be bitter toward each other regarding other issues. It works when the divorced mother and father retain a certain amount of respect for each other as parents, even though they detest each other as spouses. Finally, it works when there is some balance between the rights/prerogatives/ responsibilities of the custodial and noncustodial parents. That topic is discussed in detail in Chapter Thirteen, "Parental Rights and Responsibilities."

Joint Custody

Some judges, attorneys, and therapists have considered joint custody to be a panacea, that joint custody would be a way for divorced parents to raise the children in a cooperative manner and for both parents to think of themselves as fully involved in important decisions. In joint custody both parents have the authority to make major decisions such as enrolling the child in a particular school and giving permission

---

**Important Case: *In re the Marriage of Weidner*
(338 N.W.2d 351)**

Marvin Weidner and Betsy Weidner married in 1970 and had two children. The couple had disagreements and periods of separation. They
permanently separated in 1981. During the times of separation the children were in the primary physical custody of Betsy and she took care of
their day-to-day activities, even though both parents spent about equal
time with the children. By the time of their final separation the parties
neither trusted each other, enjoyed being in each other's company, nor
respected each other. At the divorce trial, the District Court for Polk County,
Iowa, awarded Betsy sole custody of the children.

In 1983, this case reached the Supreme Court of Iowa. The principal
issue was whether the District Court should have provided for joint custody as requested by Marvin. According to the Supreme Court of Iowa,
joint custody should be considered if it is in the best interests of the
children. In determining this, the court must consider (1) whether each
parent would be a suitable custodian for the child; (2) whether the parents can communicate with each other regarding the child's needs. In
this case, the trial court found joint custody under the circumstances
would not be conducive to a workable arrangement that would be in
the best interests of the children. While both parties seemed to be fit
and suitable to act as a custodial parent, they had not demonstrated that
they were able to communicate and give priority to the welfare of
the children by reaching shared decisions in the best interests of the
children. The Supreme Court of Iowa affirmed the decision of the lower
court agreeing that joint custody would not be feasible.

---

for major surgery. The underlying assumption in joint custody is that
major decisions will be discussed by the parents and they will try to
reach a consensus on what to do.

Even in situations where the parents have agreed to joint custody,
the actual living arrangement for the children is the same as described
above under the "traditional" plan. That is, the children usually live in
one parent's household most of the time and have regular visitation to
the other household. The fact that two parents have joint custody does
not make the task of raising the children any easier. They must still put
effort into communicating and have some degree of respect for each

other as parents. Joint custody is a good way for some divorcing parents to raise the children together. However, it is unlikely joint custody is the solution to any divorce that is extremely hostile and adversarial. This issue was addressed in an important case, *In re the Marriage of Weidner* (338 N.W.2d 351), which is summarized in the box on page 44.

Practically any arrangement works if the divorcing parents have based it on mutual respect for each other and are willing to work out the details. However, there is an important exception to the general principle that practically anything will work if both parents agree. That is, children can figure it out when parents are cooperating in an effort to achieve what is convenient for themselves rather than what is good for the children. Sometimes divorced parents agree to joint custody and then divide the children's time between the two households in a way that simply suits the convenience of the parents. The parents may be doing this because neither of them really wants to take on full responsibility for the children.

Chapter Five
Uncommon Parenting Arrangements

Mr. Stevens and Ms. Stevens had a somewhat unusual experience in the evolution of their custody arrangement. Like many divorcing parents they both desired permanent custody of all the children. They had three sons: Tom, 12; Dick, 8; and Harry, 6. Although they were not viciously angry at each other, they did fight it out in court and the judge awarded custody to the mother. The judge probably considered it a close call. The mother had been a homemaker and the primary caretaker during the marriage. However, she was chronically depressed and had even been hospitalized on one occasion when she was considered suicidal. The father was eager to raise the boys, but his time was limited because he was a successful and extremely busy architect.

What was unusual about the situation was that the oldest boy, Tom, was difficult to parent because he was impulsive, hyperactive, and had a severe learning disability. He attended a specialized school program for children with learning disabilities and emotional problems. When he was home he required a great deal of adult attention and a careful blend of both structure and nurturance. The mother had her hands full trying to raise these three boys. As a single parent it was extremely hard for her to meet the needs of the two "normal" children as well as her handicapped son. The mother's household was chaotic because there was constant friction between Tom and his mother (who found it hard to set consistent limits with him) and between Tom and his brothers (who resented how much of the mother's time he consumed). Ms. Stevens became frustrated and more depressed; Tom became dangerously impulsive; and the younger boys, Dick and Harry, felt angry and neglected.

Mr. Stevens, meanwhile, was thinking about going back to court and threatened to subpoena Ms. Stevens's psychiatrist in order to prove the mother was too disturbed to be considered a competent custodial parent. A mediator worked with the parents to see if they could find a reasonable solution without involving further litigation. The mediator helped the parents arrive at an arrangement that seemed workable: the mother would continue to be the custodial parent for Dick and Harry and the father would become the custodial parent for Tom.

This new arrangement worked out better for everybody. The father found a specialized after-school program for Tom, so he was adequately supervised. The father felt he truly had a role in raising his sons. The mother easily managed Dick and Harry and started to feel like a competent parent again. Visitation was scheduled in a way that the three siblings were frequently able to be together.

Separating the siblings into different custodial households is an uncommon outcome of custody disputes. This approach and other unusual custody arrangements will be discussed in this chapter. The message of this chapter is that there are many different circumstances in divorced families. The parents themselves may have widely different skills, attitudes, and interests when it comes to rearing children. There are many details to be considered in determining the best living arrangements for the children in a divorced family. The parameters that might be important include: the attitudes of the parents; the physical and mental health of the parents; the work schedules of the parents; the role of stepparents and extended family members; the neighborhoods where they live; the attachments the children have to the two parents; and the preferences the children may express. Since there are so many circumstances that might be important, it seems obvious there might be many different kinds of custody arrangements.

In Chapter Four and Chapter Five we have used the older terminology, referring to "custodial" and "noncustodial" parents. All of the ideas and suggestions discussed in these chapters could be implemented through the use of parenting plans, as described in Chapter Six. If that were to happen, the roles would be described as the PRP (primary residential parent) and NPRP (non-primary residential parent).

This chapter examines in detail two uncommon custody arrangements, referred to here as split custody and shared custody. Split custody is the arrangement in which siblings are separated, in that some of them primarily live with the mother and some primarily live with the father. In shared custody, both parents have legal custody of the child. However, one parent may be completely responsible for what happens during the week and the other parent is completely responsible for what happens on weekends. These custody arrangements are uncommon for a reason: most divorcing couples do fine with the traditional models discussed in Chapter Four. It is important, however, for some divorced parents to consider less common custody arrangements, such as split custody and shared custody.

Asking the Right Question

In the vignette at the beginning of this chapter the Stevenses found themselves with a tough situation. Initially they were asking themselves and also asking the court a particular question: "Is Mr. Stevens or Ms. Stevens better equipped to be the custodial parent of the three boys, Tom, Dick, and Harry?" As time went on, they were asking a different question: "How can two concerned parents, who are divorced, find a way to raise three boys, who demand an unusual degree of parental nurturing and supervision?" In the illustration, the Stevenses eventually agreed to separate the boys and divide the custody, so the father became the primary parent for Tom and the mother continued to be the primary parent for Dick and Harry.

It is unusual for parents to take that step. It is also unusual for judges to separate children in making a decision in a custody case. In some states, case law has established a presumption that siblings should stay together, so a judge would have to have a very good reason to override that legal precedent. We think in some families—although this does not occur very often—it is in the best interests of both the children and the parents for the siblings to be separated and the custody to be divided between the two parents.

Before we try to create an exception to the rule, we should try to understand why it is advantageous in most families to keep the children together. There have been several reasons for having such a strong presumption that siblings should be kept together. First of all, divorce is extremely stressful for the children. During this time in which children feel threatened, insecure, and wounded, they need all the support and consistency they can find. Many children feel more comforted and more comfortable when all the brothers and sisters are living together. They have the sense that at least part of the family is still in one piece. We agree that is an important consideration and a logical reason for keeping the children together.

The second reason for assuming siblings should stay together is also logical. That is, some siblings naturally form pairs or groups because of their gender and birth order. Two boys who are 12 and 14 years old are likely to have a great many interests in common and are likely to be extremely important to each other, even if they are fussing and feuding much of the time. It makes sense in such a family to have a presumption that the siblings would be together. In another family the children might form quite distinct groups: a divorcing couple could have two sons who are 14 and 15 and two daughters who are 7 and 8. In that family the parents might agree for the father to be the custodial parent for the boys and the mother to be the custodial parent for the girls.

Fallacious Reasoning

We can understand and support the two explanations just mentioned for keeping the siblings together. What concerns us is courts seem to go beyond those reasons and assume siblings should *always* be kept together. In being so arbitrary and so rigid, judges seem to be basing their conclusions not only on the two legitimate reasons, but on two additional fallacious reasons.

The first fallacious reason for keeping the siblings together is a result of the usual practice of creating a contest in order to figure out which parent would make the better custodial parent. When one is working within the context of a contest, the result is the winner takes everything. Think about it: if the father, for instance, is found to be a "better person" and therefore the preferred parent for child A, then he obviously is going to be the preferred parent for children B, C, and D as well. Some judges might view these situations simplistically and decide that one parent has won the case and therefore that parent should have custody of all the children. Although this reason seems superficially logical, it does not make sense. The issues in most divorced families are quite complex, and it may well be one parent will be better at raising the first child and the other parent better at raising the second child.

The second fallacious reason for keeping the siblings together is the mistaken belief that child care experts have said it should be done that way. We think some judges and therapists remember learning in school that the siblings should always be kept together in order to provide mutual support. However, they have mixed up what should be done in custody situations with what should be done in other situations when children have come to the attention of the court and require a placement decision. We are referring to unfortunate situations in which children have been orphaned, neglected, or abused and—for whatever reason—the children must be placed in foster care. Many years ago child care agencies dealt with these children like so many numbers and randomly divided them up among available foster homes. It could have happened that children from one family would be removed from both of their parents, because of abuse or neglect, and then removed from each other by placement in different foster homes. Those children would have been totally devastated, having been suddenly removed from their home, their parents, and their siblings. That kind of outcome—tragedy heaped on tragedy—does not happen so much any more because now social service agencies make efforts to keep the siblings together. Some of them have created rules or guidelines as a reminder them to keep the siblings together whenever possible.

During the last ten or twenty years the rule—"*always* keep the siblings together"—has spread from cases involving foster home placement to cases involving custody disputes. We do not think these situations are comparable. Children of divorce have not suddenly lost the love and the availability of both parents. They usually still have two devoted parents who happen to live in different homes. Even if the children live in two households, they are still going to see both parents and all their brothers and sisters on a regular schedule. Although there are reasons to keep the children of divorce together in the same custodial household, it should not be thought an absolute rule that never provides room for exceptions.

Separating the Siblings

Sometimes the arrangement in which the siblings are separated is called split custody. It should be understood that if children are divided between two parents, the children continue to be together in the same household more than half the time. The visitation schedule between the two homes can be arranged so the children are together five days out of seven. The typical schedule for a school-aged child is to visit the noncustodial parent every other weekend, from Friday evening to Sunday evening, and also one weekday evening every week. The example that follows of John and Mary shows how it would turn out if a divorced couple decided to divide the custody of their children. For the sake of simplicity, we will say that the father has custody of John and the mother has custody of Mary.

The location of the two children over a two-week period of time is summarized in the box on the page 51. In our example, Mary had her weekend visit with the father on the first weekend. John had his weekend visit with the mother on the second weekend. In addition to the every other weekend visitation, they have agreed that John visits the

Residential Schedule When Siblings Are Divided

	Dad's House	Mom's House
Monday	John	Mary
Tuesday	John, Mary	
Wednesday		John, Mary
Thursday	John	Mary
Friday	John, Mary	
Saturday	John, Mary	
Sunday	John, Mary	
Monday	John	Mary
Tuesday	John, Mary	
Wednesday		John, Mary
Thursday	John	Mary
Friday		John, Mary
Saturday		John, Mary
Sunday		John, Mary

This table shows that John and Mary would be together most of the time, even though they primarily live in different households.

mother's home every Wednesday evening and that Mary visits the father's home every Tuesday evening. By arranging the schedule in a reciprocal manner, the children are actually living together in the same household every single weekend and two evenings during the week. The only waking times during which they would routinely be away from each other are Monday evenings and Thursday evenings. In fact, that result is not a bad outcome, because it makes sense to allow each child to have some individual time with a parent in addition to their time together.

Shared Custody

Another uncommon custody arrangement is what we call shared custody. In some ways it is similar to joint custody, but it has features that may be important in situations where traditional joint custody does not work. In shared custody, one parent is completely in charge of school activities and the child lives with that parent on weekdays. The second parent is completely in charge of church and other events, such as the child's participation in weekend Little League. The parents are not expected to seek the other person's opinion or agreement, since each parent has the authority to make the decisions regarding his or her area of responsibility.

Shared custody, as described here, is not appropriate for most divorcing parents. If the two parents communicate well with each other and respect each other's opinions and feelings, then they might adjust better with traditional joint custody. If one parent is clearly a better choice because that parent is much more competent or has a much better relationship with the child, it would probably be better to have the common arrangement of a custodial and a noncustodial parent.

Shared custody should be considered if both parents have significant strengths and weaknesses and if neither parent appears ready and able to take full responsibility for the child. Also, this arrangement should be considered if both parents need to take a major share of child-rearing responsibility, but are not willing to communicate and confer with each other. For example, shared parenting should be considered if one parent happens to be very good at monitoring the child's school work in an orderly and helpful manner and if the other parent happens to be very good at creating and supervising recreational activities. Further, shared custody should be considered if the parents both work and have complementary schedules, such that one parent always works during the week and the other one always works on weekends.

Anything Goes . . . Almost

Practically any arrangement works if the divorcing parents have taken three important issues into consideration. First, the plan should be derived primarily from the needs of the children rather than from the schedule that is most convenient for the parents. Second, the parents should have some sense of mutual respect for each other, rather than feeling that one parent is trying to take advantage of the other. Finally, it is important to communicate to work out the details.

Divorcing parents have devised many custody and visitation plans that may seem unusual. For example:

- Some parents have retained the family home, and each parent also rented a small apartment for his or her own use. In other words,

---

An Unusual Parenting Plan

Mom was dating two men—who did not know about each other—when she became pregnant and ultimately gave birth to a baby boy. Mom told both Dad-1 and Dad-2 that he was the father and for two years she arranged visitation time for both of them. That apparently worked well until Mom announced she was going to marry another man and move out of the state. Both Dad-1 and Dad-2 independently filed for custody of "his" child. At that point, Dad-1 and Dad-2 found out about each other. It was arranged for everybody to have blood tests to determine the child's paternity—and it was discovered that the child's father was . . . Dad-3, another man altogether!

---

the children continued to live all the time in exactly the same place. During most of the week the custodial parent lived with the children in the family home and the noncustodial parent lived in his apartment. During visitation times the custodial parent stayed in her apartment and the noncustodial parent lived with the children in the family home.

- Rather than have weekend visitation, some parents have agreed that the children would live with the custodial parent for three weeks straight and then with the noncustodial parent for one full week. That would work if the parents live near each other and it is convenient to go to school and to other regular activities from both households.

- In another family the children lived in each household half the time. That is, they lived six months with one parent and then six months with the other parent. Of course, during both halves of the year the children had visitation with the parent they were not living with.

- Unusual visitation schedules also occur when the parents live in distant cities. The parents might agree that the children would spend the entire school year with one parent and the winter vacation and summer vacation with the other parent.

These unusual custody and visitation arrangements work because parents go into them with both eyes open and with some willingness to cooperate and negotiate with the former spouse. In our experience, courts approve almost any arrangement that has been worked out between the parents unless the schedule was obviously harmful to the children. We heard about an uncommon visitation arrangement that was so bizarre it had to undone and resolved by the court. See the box on page 53.

Disclaimer

Divorcing parents can choose among a wide range of custody arrangements for their children. Some of the custody plans discussed in Chapter Four and in this chapter are quite different from each other. The point is that parents, attorneys, and judges should think about these issues in creative ways that are adapted to each family's individual situation.

Our disclaimer is that we are not trying to suggest that any custody or visitation system at all is going to work smoothly. Parents have come up with ideas that are very impracticable. Courts have been known to impose unusual custody plans and certain restrictions on visitation that are doomed to fail because: they are extremely arbitrary; they give an unusual advantage to one of the parents; or they ignore the developmental needs of the children. For instance, one judge stated a noncustodial parent could have visitation with his children absolutely any weekend he wanted, as long as he gave 60 days notice to the custodial parent. The problem was the noncustodial parent was in the military and it was very hard for him to plan far in advance; on some occasions he planned the visit three months ahead, but was not granted leave when the actual weekend arrived.

Chapter Four and Chapter Five described four types of custody arrangements: the traditional plan with the custodial parent and the noncustodial parent; joint custody, in which both parents have legal authority to make decisions; split custody, in which siblings live in different primary households; and shared custody, in which each parent has primary responsibility for different parts of the child's life. All of these arrangements could be brought about by the decision of a judge after hearing two weeks of emotional testimony. Or, these arrangements could be brought about by means of a parenting plan, which the parents have discussed and developed and negotiated between themselves. The concept of the parenting plan is discussed in the next chapter.

Chapter Six
Parent Education and Parenting Plans

Jeanette and Howard Thompson met while attending a large state university, fell in love, and married. They had two sons. Jeanette was an attractive—almost glamorous—woman who enjoyed an active social calendar. Howard, a busy and successful insurance salesman, preferred to stay at home. Although they both loved their sons, Jeanette and Howard grew apart and no longer loved each other. Somewhat reluctantly, they agreed to divorce.

As the divorce process built up steam, the parents' friends and relatives encouraged them to start cataloguing and documenting their criticisms of each other. That was not so hard to do. For example, Jeanette went to rehab several years previously for cocaine abuse and Howard had a brief affair with a woman who worked in his office. They both hired attorneys. Jeanette hired a male attorney who was known to fight hard for women's rights. Howard had the idea it would look good to have a female attorney. It turned out that both attorneys were quite competent and they both tried to avoid expensive, unnecessary trials.

After meeting with their respective clients, the attorneys knew both Jeanette and Howard were perfectly nice people and capable parents. It was obvious they both loved their sons; as far as the attorneys could tell, the boys loved both their parents. With the parents' permission, the attorneys got together and worked out a tentative plan for how Jeanette and Howard could raise the boys in a cooperative manner. The details are not important for this anecdote, but it was agreed that the children would spend most of the weekdays with their mother and most of the week-ends and holidays with their father. Although we are not suggesting that everyone in the family lived happily ever after, it was clear years later the boys had strong, positive relationships with both of their parents.

Parent Education

Many jurisdictions now require divorcing parents to attend and complete a parent education seminar. Most of these programs last four hours, but some may continue for as long as twelve hours. Parent education programs usually occur in a classroom setting with one or two instructors and 15 to 20 "students." The format of some programs resembles a support group meeting. Some instructors encourage divorcing couples to attend the same seminar series; other instructors prefer parents to attend different seminars.

Parent education seminars can be beneficial for divorcing parents, never-married parents, previously divorced parents who are modifying parenting agreements, grandparents, and concerned family members. The purpose of these educational programs is multifaceted. They are a perfect way for parents to gain a better understanding of the court process, the use of parenting plans, and the importance of mediation regarding difficult issues. Parents may even learn about alternatives to divorce. Many people have absolutely no experience with the legal system, the court process, or options such as mediation. Parent education programs effectively explain the roles and expectations of the various people involved in the divorce process. This kind of education is helpful when the individual parties subsequently consult with their attorneys.

As people go through divorce they suffer many psychological reactions and parent education plays an important role in explaining these reactions. Divorcing parents learn about the emotional upheavals they will face during the next year or so. The experience of separation and divorce is truly a grief process that can be divided into five phases: denial, anger, bargaining, depression, and acceptance. Divorcing parents need to recognize their transition through these stages as well as develop stress management techniques to deal with these painful times.

There are also serious economic changes in divorce. It is critical for both parents to analyze the long-term aspects of ending their relationship, being careful to give appropriate weight to the positive and negative aspects of the pending divorce and how their separated families are going to handle these challenges. A home divided cannot live on the same budget as it did prior to a divorce. Even with child support and alimony, there will be important financial consequences when parents live in separate homes.

"Children in the Middle"

The Center for Divorce Education developed a curriculum called "Children in the Middle: Divorce Education for Parents." This program has been identified by the Substance Abuse and Mental Health Services Administration (SAMSA) as a "model program" resulting in less subsequent litigation by the participants.

This program is unusual because it involves both parents and children. The parent group watches a video featuring realistic scenes portrayed by actual families of divorce, which show appropriate and inappropriate methods of handling conflict. The children's program uses a different, child-focused video and workbook exercises.

Information about this and other products from the Center for Divorce Education is available at www.divorce-educaton.com.

Relationships among friends and extended families also change. Divorcing parents often find that family members and friends choose sides or stay away altogether because of their lack of understanding or lack of comfort with the process. The parent education seminars can help with all of these adjustments.

Divorce is a period of transition. A thorough examination of feelings and frustrations during this time aids the parties in adjusting to the change in lifestyle. The typical parent education course also provides parents with advice as to how to assist their children in coping with the divorce. Many parents do not recognize the traumatic effect divorce has on the children. The children endure the same phases of loss previously mentioned and parents need to be aware of these stages and react appropriately. These seminars are an excellent opportunity to gain an understanding of the child's reactions and emotions. Children suffer differently based upon their ages and specific situations. A parenting education seminar can help parents adjust their reactions to accommodate each of their children's needs. In the parent education seminars, parents learn new approaches to discipline, receive guidelines for discussing divorce with their children, and develop skills to help their children through the transition to different living arrangements.

It is also anticipated that new family structures are a possibility, which may eventually include stepparents. Well over half of divorcing parents will get remarried. It is important for parents to understand how the introduction of new people into their children's lives can cause great stress or great benefit. Knowledge about these issues is always the key to successful parenting of children of divorce.

The next phase of the parenting education program is usually the "looking forward" portion. This part explains several areas, such as helping friends and family cope with the divorce and changing the parent's environment. Information is given about seeking further help when necessary, such as individual counseling or group therapy. The parenting seminar should provide resource materials and contacts to assist divorcing parents and their children. Divorce is a traumatic experience and any education the parties can receive during this difficult stage is important in becoming better parents.

In some seminars, a screen for domestic violence is administered. If violence is detected, the abused parent requires immediate help. He or she also should advise their legal counsel, because mediation may not be appropriate in these circumstances.

Children's Rights

An important topic for parent education programs and for anyone developing a parenting plan is the concept of children's rights. Children have rights in a divorce, just like the parents. Many lists of children's rights can be found on the Internet or by perusing parenting self-help books. On page 59 is a list of children's rights developed by Families First, a social service agency that has been active in Atlanta, Georgia, for more than one hundred years.

Parenting Plans

In 1996, the U.S. Commission on Child and Family Welfare made recommendations that would significantly change the way divorced parents raise their children. The Commission shifted the focus from "custody" to "parenting plans." Both of these concepts emphasize that children of divorced parents should be nurtured and raised by both the mother and the father. Although both "custody" and "parenting plans" can result in good child-rearing practices, there are differences in the implications of these terms. The concept of legal custody emphasizes the legal end result, that is, the court has ordered the parents to share certain rights and responsibilities, but one parent is primarily responsible for raising the child. The concept of parenting plans emphasizes

Children's Rights in Divorce

I have the right . . .

- *To be told my mother and my father will always love me.*
- *To be told the family breakup is not my fault.*
- *To be seen as a human being and not a piece of property to be fought for or bargained over.*
- *To have decisions about me be based upon what is in my best interests and not my parents' hurt feelings or needs.*
- *To love both my father and my mother without being forced to choose or feel guilty.*
- *To know both my mother and my father through regular and frequent involvement in my life.*
- *To have the financial support of both my mother and my father.*
- *To be spared from hearing hurtful or negative comments about either of my parents.*
- *To be a child and not asked to lie, spy, or send messages between my parents.*
- *To be allowed to have affection for new people who come into my life without feeling guilty or being pressured.*

the process by which divorcing parents sit down, talk to each other, and work out an agreement regarding their child's future.

Several states (for example, Colorado, Missouri, Oregon, Tennessee, Washington, and West Virginia) have adopted some form of parenting plans. In these states, marital dissolution agreements, which include provisions for child custody, are usually replaced by the submission of parenting plans. These new laws have emphasized shared parenting or co-parenting. In some states, the terms "custodial parent" and "noncustodial parent" are no longer used. Instead, the laws use terms such as "primary residential parent" and "non-primary residential parent." Rather than referring to "visitation," these laws use the term "parenting time."

In states using parenting plans, divorcing parents are encouraged to work out a detailed agreement between themselves. If the parents are unable to accomplish that task on their own, they are expected to make use of mediation. If the parents together with a mediator cannot agree on a parenting plan, the dispute will then be addressed in the traditional manner—in a courtroom with a judge making the final decisions.

The underlying premise of parenting plans is that raising children is a long-term responsibility and parents should focus on that task instead of the painful relationship with the divorcing spouse. "Custody" and "visitation" seem to be mere buzzwords for continued conflict between divorcing parents. The traditional language of "custodial" and "noncustodial" parent may have promoted distancing one parent's relationship with the child in comparison to the other parent. Children are not one's personal property. Children are not just one parent's responsibility. Both parents working together, though they are no longer intimate partners, can still raise well-adjusted children as long as that goal remains their combined focus.

The purpose of parenting plans is to plan effectively for the long-term best interests of the child. Parenting plans are superior to other forms of custody determination because they are more specific and the parents arrive at an agreement jointly, which hopefully reduces the risk of confusion or conflict in the future. Each parenting plan should reflect the personal choices of the two people in charge of rearing their children and should address the changing needs of the children as much as possible. Who better knows the day-to-day needs of their children than the parents? A parenting plan helps the mother and father think about what is best for the long-term well being of the children early in the divorce process.

Most divorcing parents need some help in developing a parenting plan. In some cases the parents' two attorneys help them work out the details. In other cases, the parents might need the assistance of a divorce mediator. Normally, parenting plans are divided into the following five sections.

Financial and Administrative Provisions

This section specifies whether one parent will pay child support to the other parent; which parent receives the income tax exemption; and provisions for health insurance, dental insurance, and life insurance.

Schedules

The plan usually has separate provisions for each person's parenting time schedule during preschool years; the parenting time schedule during elementary, middle, and high school (as well as the names of the schools, if known, and who is going to pay for it); the schedule for winter, spring, and summer vacations; the schedule for holidays; and transportation arrangements.

Decision-Making

The parents agree on whether one or both parents have responsibility for making routine day-to-day decisions as well as major decisions regarding education, religious upbringing (including which parent will take the child to services and religious education), extracurricular activities, and healthcare (including the name of the pediatrician, who is able to authorize medical care, and who pays for it). Of course, the focus of the parenting plan should remain the best interests of the child. Simply, each parent should search for choices that are the least disruptive upon the child's life. It is important to develop a plan through which both parents participate actively and are supportive of the other's activities in child rearing.

Dispute Resolution

Since it is possible that disagreements between the parents will occur in the future after the divorce proceedings are concluded, the parents agree ahead of time on how the disputes will be resolved. For example, they may specify the use of counseling, mediation, or arbitration. In some states, mediators can be family members, clergy, or a person whom the parties have used in the past to help solve difficulties. Both parties should agree to the mediator and the method. Using this alternative type of dispute resolution will save time, energy, money, and heartache for each parent. One of the many advantages of using a mediator is his or her ability to keep the parties focused on the best interests of the child at a time of emotional volatility.

Standard Rights

The parenting plan may specify that both parents have certain rights, whether or not the child is currently with that parent, such as: unimpeded telephone conversations with the child; educational information from the child's school; and medical information from the child's physician.

There are a number of goals that should be accomplished during discussion and development of a parenting plan. The basic purpose of the parenting plan concept is to provide a more humane, thoughtful, and private alternative to the adversarial process and permit self-determination. Secondly, it is very useful as a negotiation model for the parents and should remove the negative atmosphere and establish a business-like relationship. Thirdly, it removes legal jargon and replaces it with common everyday terms to set the framework for family reorganization. Next, it develops a minimum standard or baseline with which the parents can start their work toward the long-term best interests of the children. Lastly, as previously stated and again emphasized, the parenting plan process encourages both parents to make the children their number one priority and recognize the children's need to maintain close continuous relationships with both the mother and the father. When developing these documents, parents should work on a plan that will bring a benefit to the child versus one more convenient for the parents.

Parenting plans are not set in stone. Parenting plans should be flexible documents that both parties can modify at any time they agree to do so. The form itself can easily constitute an agreed order when modifications become necessary. In times past, judges simply assigned custody to one parent and ordered "liberal and reasonable visitation" to the other parent. That approach, which is now outdated, does not work for the long-term good of the children and may cause difficulties for many years after the divorce is final. Our children deserve better, and parenting plans—which are developed both thoroughly and sincerely—are a good approach for the future. Having considered the general principles of divorce and parenting plans, we now move on to the day-to-day and week-to-week details of raising and nurturing the children of divorce.

Chapter Seven
Balancing the Needs of
Parents and Children

Two parents, who were both successful professionals, consulted a thera-pist who was experienced in custody and visitation evaluations. The par-ents were in the process of divorcing and said that they both wanted to do what was best for their two daughters, Merrie and Melodie. Merrie was 16 and Melodie was 12. They both expressed the lofty view that they did not want to take the other parent to court and have a big custody battle, but they wanted to work out what was best for the girls in a rational and cooperative manner. They both were concerned the girls were already distraught over the divorce and were manifesting symp-toms. Merrie was acting out sexually and Melodie was depressed and alluding to suicidal ideation.

The parents explained the plan they had already worked out be-tween themselves. Both parents had important careers and both wanted to continue to work full time. They had agreed on a schedule in which both daughters would alternate between the mother's household and the father's household on a weekly basis. They had agreed on joint custody, so each parent would be fully responsible for the girls when they were with that parent.

The therapist interviewed Merrie and Melodie separately and also together. They both were angry and miserable. They strongly resented the arrangement in which they had to live in two different households. The girls did not seem distressed about the divorce itself. They had strong attachments to both parents and were perfectly willing to live with either their mother or father. What they resented was having to live half the time in each household. They had figured out that the parents were put-ting their own convenience above the needs of the girls.

The therapist met again with the parents and determined the basic issue in the case, that neither parent was willing to take charge of the situation and to provide a full-time home for their daughters. Both par-ents really wanted the other parent to take full responsibility of Merrie and Melodie. The therapist explained his assessment of the girls, that their symptoms were related to feeling neglected and being repeatedly displaced on a week-to-week basis. The therapist was able to propose some other options for the parents to consider. One possibility was the traditional arrangement of one parent working only part-time and being able to raise the children. The parent who continued to work full-time would, of course, provide child support. A second possibility was for the girls to alternate on a much longer cycle, such as every six months or once a year. A third possibility was for each parent to be the primary parent for one child. That is, Merrie could live with the father and visit the mother; Melodie could live with the mother and visit the father.

This chapter is about parents who avoid their basic responsibilities to the children. They are putting their own needs above the needs of the children. The usual scenario in custody and visitation disputes is one or both parents are attempting to take something away from the other parent. That is, Parent A is trying to take custody away from Parent B or attempting to limit Parent B's visitation. In the family of Merrie and Melodie, however, both parents were trying to push more visitation and more responsibility off onto the other parent. Merrie and Melodie were the victims of a reverse custody dispute.

Sometimes the phenomenon of the reverse custody dispute is apparent to all. It is like O. Henry's famous story, "The Ransom of Red Chief." Kidnappers abducted a very demanding and very obnoxious little boy who was the son a wealthy banker. The child was so disagreeable the kidnappers eventually were willing to pay the father to take the child back.

In the case of Merrie and Melodie the process was more subtle. In fact, what was interesting was the disguise the mother and father had developed. The parents had colluded in a way to look like they were only concerned about the girls' welfare, that is, for the girls to have a continuing relationship with both mother and father. In fact, what the parents really had in mind was to avoid providing what the girls needed, a consistent household.

Divorced parents may find many ways to put their own interests and needs above those of the children. As far as they are concerned, divorce means to find a way to achieve "the best interests of the parents." The reverse custody dispute is one way in which the parents maneuver to take less responsibility for the children. This chapter will describe both blatant and subtle ways in which parents neglect their children's needs.

Blatant Neglect by Divorced Parents

It is fortunately uncommon to meet parents who actively shun responsibility for their children. It may happen, however, when a parent is irresponsible and puts personal desires and convenience above the needs of the child. A parent who has a serious alcohol or drug problem may be temporarily oblivious to the physical safety and other needs of the child. On the other hand, a single parent may not be irresponsible, but just overwhelmed. For instance, a parent might find an unusually difficult child to be emotionally draining and may eventually tune out the child's requests for nurturance, for attention, and simply for dinner.

A divorced individual may find the demands of an active social life may compromise his or her responsibilities as a parent. This criticism is made more often about mothers. A divorced mother may very much want to develop a relationship with a new boyfriend. She may invite the boyfriend to move in with her. She may end up with a long series of boyfriends who have become roommates. The children in her household would certainly be bumped to the bottom of her list of priorities.

Another rather blatant form of neglect is to include the children in the parent's partying. This seems to happen more with single parents, perhaps because two parents who are together are more likely to police each other. In any case, what happens is that friends congregate at the parent's home and the partying gets under way. Under the best of these circumstances, the children are passive observers of the grown-ups' activities. When the situation deteriorates further, the adults may give drugs to the children and make them vulnerable to sexual abuse.

The Disappearing Parent

An NPRP (non-primary residential parent) may neglect his or her children by disappearing—a ruthlessly clear message that the parent considers his or her needs more important than what might be good for the child. When a psychiatrist or psychologist conducts a custody evaluation, he may ask both parents what they will do if the court decides the case in favor of the other parent. One time a mother said that if she lost the custody battle she would move to Oregon and never see her children again. The evaluator thought she might have misunderstood the question, so he asked her again. She assured the evaluator she was convinced that if she could not have total control of her children, she had no interest in having any relationship with them at all. For anybody who reads this book and happens to see a mental health professional for a psychiatric custody evaluation, that was the *wrong answer*. The mother's response graphically displayed how her own emotional needs were more important than her relationship with the children.

On another occasion, a psychiatrist conducted a custody evaluation and testified on behalf of the mother. In comparing the psychological fitness of the two parents, the evaluator thought the mother was more nurturing and was a more consistent caretaker for the child, a little boy. The evaluator stated that in court, and the judge agreed and ordered custody to the mother and regular visitation for the father. The father complained that he had been described as "not particularly nurturing." Two weeks later the father proved beyond a reasonable doubt that he did not have nurturing attitudes toward his son. It was time for his scheduled visitation with his son and the father simply did not show up. In fact, the father did not show up for three months because he was so angry the judge did not make him the primary custodian of his son.

Sadly, many NPRP parents do drop out of sight. They move away, perhaps remarry, and move on with their lives in a way that does not include their children. What seems worse is the NPRP parent who intermittently disappears, but surfaces often enough to tease the child in a mean-spirited way. These parents have a way of telephoning a few weeks before Christmas or before the child's birthday and promising that some special present is going to arrive for the child. The child, of course, gets his hopes up and then is disappointed over and over.

Subtle Neglect by Divorced Parents

Most of the time divorced parents are not so obvious in the way they neglect their children's needs. In fact, sometimes this form of "neglect" actually takes on the appearance of almost limitless affection and concern for the child.

For example, what about the NPRP, a mother in this instance, who seems extremely concerned about how her son Randolph is doing in the second grade? The mother's home is not the child's primary residence and she misses him. The mother senses that Randolph is dearly missing her also and she feels the need to comfort him frequently. In order to check on his schoolwork and to make sure he isn't missing her too much, the mother starts to phone Randolph every evening around dinnertime. By every evening, we mean *every* evening. Since she wants to make sure he gets off to a good day in school, she starts calling

Randolph in the mornings when he is having breakfast. Since she wants
him to do his best in school, the mother starts checking with the teacher
every week or so. Under the guise of being a nurturing, concerned
mother, she may well be hurting Randolph more than helping him. In
particular, it is likely she is missing Randolph more than Randolph is
missing her. The real purpose of the phone calls is for the mother's
reassurance rather than for the child's. What Randolph really needs to
hear from his mother is he is a good boy and he can get along without
her for several days or even a week at a time. The way to get that idea
across to Randolph is to stop calling him every day.

Or what about the NPRP, a father, who decides it is his mission in
life to turn his 12-year-old son, Macon, into a premier student-athlete?
The father starts to attend every basketball practice and every game.
He sits near the bench so he can give reminders to Macon when he is
not actually playing. The father enrolls the boy in the Saturday Scholar
program at the local university, so he can get a head start in computer
programming. And for the rest of the weekend they practice together to
be ready for the father-son handball tournament. Is this merely a dedicated father? Or is this a man who is taking advantage of his son and
using the boy to give the father some sense of fulfillment?

Balancing the Needs of Parents and Children

It is easy to criticize parents who are divorced and are trying to
balance their own needs as single and perhaps insecure parents with
the needs of their children. The basic message here is *not* that divorced
parents should be totally selfless in raising their children. The message
is *not* that divorced parents should be perfect in resolving the complex
issues that come up almost every day. The message is something like
this: raising children is very hard work; it is even harder when the
parents are divorced; parents do have to expect to make some sacrifices;
divorced parents should strive to find a balance between their own needs
as adults and their children's needs; and, especially, parents should not
fool themselves into thinking their decisions and their behaviors are in
the children's interests when actually they are serving the emotional
needs of the parents.

Here are some ways to balance the needs of parents and children.
The following suggestions and examples involve some degree of conflict
between the interests of the parent and the needs of the child. There is
no simple answer to some of these scenarios. The purpose of these ex-

amples is not to give cookbook advice for how to deal with complex situations, but to illustrate several ways by which a person might balance these conflicting interests.

• Divorced parents may find it more convenient to deal with their children as a group, all at the same time. Children, however, benefit from sharing some individual time with each parent. One way to accomplish this is to take one child out to do some shopping, while the other child plays at a friend's house. Visitation might be arranged so that, on some occasions, the NPRP only has one child at a time. This requires a greater time commitment by both parents, but it is better for the children.

• Being a single parent can be lonely. It is a common problem for single parents to use their children as buddies, confidants, and soulmates. In one family, a divorced mother was concerned about her son and only child, who was a high school senior. Although a bright student who had previously done well in school, the youngster was foundering and it looked like he would not be able to go away to college and might not even graduate from high school on time. The mother and boy spent much of their free time together. Their Saturday evening routine was dinner and the theater. A counselor explained firmly that the mother and son needed to separate from each other in the psychological sense. As a starter, they needed to have separate social lives. The mother and boy agreed they depended too much on each other. After achieving some emotional distance from his mother, the boy did well in school and went away to college.

• When they plan for holidays, divorced parents should think of the needs of the children. That does not refer to purchasing a pile of presents and having a bang-up holiday dinner. When the kids arrive for a Christmas holiday, for example, let them relax and unwind and simply hang out for a while, rather than hustling them off immediately to see the relatives. Holiday celebrations require a lot of preparation and parents sometimes expect children to demonstrate their appreciation in an explicit manner, such as saying, "Thank you very much," after each present is opened. It is better for a parent to feel satisfied and appreciated by simply enjoying a good time together with his children, rather than waiting for all those thank you's.

• In Los Angeles, divorced parents had an adult son who had cystic fibrosis. Cystic fibrosis is a chronic illness that gradually destroyed the son's lungs. In fact, he was near death. In an unusual operation,

---

Biological vs. Psychological Parent

Although it is generally agreed that in a custody dispute everybody should be working toward the best interests of the child, life is not always so simple. Frequently courts must consider the legal rights of the biological parents and the rights of the psychological parents (who might be somebody else), as well as the child's best interests.

A dramatic example of such a problem was the dispute between Daniel and Cara Schmidt, who lived in Iowa, and Jan and Roberta DeBoer, who lived in Michigan. Their little girl was the biological child of the Schmidts, but she had lived since birth with the DeBoers. The DeBoers were undoubtedly the girl's psychological parents. The courts in both states thought the rights of the biological parents should be taken into consideration, even if those rights may conflict with the best interests of the child.

The concept of the psychological parent was explained in an important book, *Beyond the Best Interests of the Child* (Free Press, 1973), which was written by Joseph Goldstein, Anna Freud, and Albert Solnit. The same authors wrote *Before the Best Interests of the Child* (Free Press, 1979) and *In the Best Interests of the Child* (with Sonja Goldstein) (Free Press, 1986).

---

surgeons transplanted parts of the lungs of both parents into their son's chest in order to save his life. According to a newspaper report, the parents, who had divorced 17 years previously, held hands on the way to the surgery. Most divorced parents do not have such dramatic roles to play, but they still struggle with how to balance their personal needs with their child's welfare.

•   There may be an irreconcilable conflict between the legitimate rights of parents and the bests interests of the child. This can happen when one or both of the biological parents have been separated from the child for some reason that was beyond their control. The courts must resolve these difficult cases. See the box on this page for an example.

The most important consideration in providing for the emotional needs of children of divorce is to protect the child from parental battles. Parents may need to be less demanding and less self-centered in order to avoid fighting over the children, through the children, and in front of the children. Another consideration is to find a balance between the needs of the children and the needs of the parents. Happily, many times children and their parents need exactly the same thing, but often it is necessary to work out compromises and set priorities. Finally, it may be quite challenging to help the child have loving and satisfying relationships with both parents. That is the subject of the next chapter, "Trying to Love Both Parents."

Chapter Eight
Trying To Love Both Parents

Annie and Danny were young teenagers who lived with their father. Their parents had divorced when they were in elementary school. The father had obtained permanent custody of both children at the time, primarily because the mother was having some medical problems that prevented her from putting very much energy into the rearing of the two active, boisterous, and somewhat demanding children.

When her health improved, the mother went back to court and requested that both children be transferred to her custody. She had a vigorous attorney who argued there had been a change of circumstance, that is, the mother's health had improved and she was now available to be a fully competent full-time parent. The attorney also argued since the mother was not employed, she was even more available than the father to nurture and supervise Annie and Danny. Finally, the attorney learned that Danny had been in counseling and he subpoenaed the therapist's notes. The attorney discovered the counseling had started because there had been some conflict between Danny and his father, so this provided even more ammunition for the mother's case.

The legal process went on for about six months, from the time the mother originally filed her custody suit to the time the court made its decision to leave Annie and Danny in the custody of their father. The court felt it was better to leave well enough alone because the children seemed to be thriving in the father's household; because they were behaving about as well as young adolescents usually behave; and because both children expressed a preference to leave the custody arrangement the way it had been.

During the six months of legal wrangling, the family's activities remained the same. The children were living with the father and had regular visitation with the mother, every other weekend from Friday evening to Sunday evening. Annie and Danny enjoyed riding and grooming the horse the mother kept. The children and the mother had created a tradition of seeing every new horror movie at the local multiplex theater, which

71

they all enjoyed. During that time, however, Danny became less enthusi-
astic about planning activities for the visitation. He started to find rea-
sons to postpone the visitations or return home early. He stopped initiat-
ing phone calls to his mother and he seemed to lack interest in pleasing
her or spending time with her. Several months after the court case ended,
Danny refused to visit his mother at all.

With that turn of events, Danny was taken again to see his therapist.
The therapist was puzzled because there was no obvious reason for the
boy's intense alienation from his mother. Had the mother intimidated or
pressured him during the court case? Danny said no. Had either parent
been saying bad things about the other parent? The youngster did not
describe any form of bad-mouthing or indoctrination, but simply said
that he was aware of the anger and tension between the parents. Had the
father been suggesting, even in a subtle manner, that Danny did not need
to visit the mother so often? No, said Danny. In fact, the father had
persistently encouraged both children to continue the visitation at the
scheduled times every other weekend. As the therapist got a little more
desperate to find an explanation for Danny's refusal of visitation, he
started to wonder if the boy had been traumatized in some way, but had
kept it secret. He eventually came right out and asked if Danny had been
physically abused or sexually molested at the mother's home, which the
boy denied. The therapist even investigated if the child could have been
hypnotized by the father, which seemed unlikely.

Danny's refusal to visit his mother was stated adamantly, but was
supported by vague explanations. The child simply said he had other
more important things to do, he did not particularly enjoy being with his
mother, he didn't think that she understood him, she didn't treat him
right, he didn't see any point to having a relationship with his mother,
and so on. Danny's explanations were vague because he himself did not
really understand what had happened to him. His subjective experience
was simply that he had a perfectly good relationship with his father and
he did not find it pleasant to spend time with his mother.

The story about Danny illustrates something that happens often
enough, that a child of divorced parents becomes strongly alienated from
one of the parents, usually the NPRP (non-primary residential parent).
For the child, the affection he has for the "alienated parent" is about the
same as he feels for some distant relative or for some neighbor down
the street. He does not experience a sense of attachment and he finds
that parent's expressions of affection to be intrusive and annoying.

What is this phenomenon and why does it happen? Therapists and attorneys who work with divorced parents and their children have seen many examples of this condition, which often are more heart-breaking than the story about Danny. The usual explanation for parental alienation is the custodial parent has actively brainwashed the child into disliking the other parent. We are sure that indoctrination does happen in some divorced families and it leads to parental alienation. However, we think there is another explanation for this condition, which does not involve indoctrination at all. Basically, it is very hard for a child to love both parents when he knows the parents are angrily fighting with each other. Both of these methods for arriving at parent alienation will be discussed in this chapter.

The terms of "indoctrination" and "parental alienation" are both somewhat pejorative. They both suggest there has been a malicious person who has actively induced the child to dislike one of the parents. The former term certainly requires that someone actually did the indoctrination. The latter term suggests someone actively alienated the child from one of the parents. A more neutral way to think about parental alienation is simply to think of the child as having already made up his mind. The child who has completely made up his mind about his feelings about his parents may have been influenced by an active, malicious process ("parental alienation through indoctrination") or may have been influenced by his exposure to specific adversarial conditions ("parental alienation without indoctrination").

Parental Alienation Through Indoctrination

This process is quite easy to understand and is sometimes easy to detect. It may occur when one parent is still very angry at her former spouse and she takes advantage of her role as the PRP to induce the child to criticize and dislike the NPRP. Since the PRP has almost total control over what the child hears, thinks, and feels, she can use her power to help the child believe that she is a wonderful parent and the father is a bum. (Please do not assume that mothers do this any more than fathers, just because this section is written with feminine pronouns. This material is easier to follow if we consistently refer to the PRP as the mother.)

Most indoctrination is done in a fairly subtle manner. We doubt that the mother simply sits the child down and says, "I want you to hate

Controversy Regarding Richard A. Gardner, M.D.

Richard A. Gardner, M.D., was a child psychiatrist who helped to identify and define the parental alienation syndrome. He published several books related to this subject, including *Psychotherapy With Children of Divorce* (Jason Aronson, 1991) and *The Parental Alienation Syndrome* (Creative Therapeutics, 1992).

Dr. Gardner said parental alienation is characterized by eight features:

- Campaign of denigration
- Weak, frivolous, or absurd rationalization for the denigration
- Lack of ambivalence
- Independent thinker phenomenon
- Reflexive support of the alienating parent
- Absence of guilt
- Borrowed scenarios
- Spread of animosity to extended family and friends

Dr. Gardner divided the cases of parental alienation syndrome into three types—mild, moderate, and severe—and that determination helps the therapist know what approach to use in counseling. For extensive information about parental alienation syndrome, see *The International Handbook of Parental Alienation Syndrome: Conceptual, Clinical and Legal Considerations*, edited by Richard A. Gardner, Richard S. Sauber, and Demosthenes Lorandos (Charles C. Thomas, 2006).

There is a good deal of controversy regarding the work of Dr. Gardner and the concept of parental alienation syndrome. Almost all mental health professionals who work with children of divorce would agree that some children in high conflict divorces become alienated from one of the parents, but they do not think this process should be called a "syndrome." Also, there is concern that some parents may misuse the concept of parental alienation syndrome in court to gain an unfair advantage over the other parent.

Daddy because he is wicked." What actually happens is probably more low-key and takes place over a period of time. The mother might make many statements which seem to be supportive and sympathetic to the beleaguered child and suggest a special relationship between the child and the mother. For instance:

"I'm sorry Daddy spanked you at his house yesterday. Let me give you a big hug."

"It's too bad you have to spend Christmas with Daddy's family. You remember what your grandmother said to you last year."

"I'm going to miss you so much when you're at Daddy's house for the weekend. Be sure to call me Saturday evening to make sure that I'm okay."

"Did Daddy hurt your peepee when he gave you a bath last night? I hope he wasn't mean to you."

Keep up those comments for a few weeks and you will probably have a child who feels her mother is the only person in the world who really loves her; who is convinced her father is a mean, violent, dangerous person to be feared and avoided; and who has concluded the only course of action is to become oppositional and hysterical when her father comes to pick her up for visitation. Even more manipulations can take place when stepparents are introduced into the picture. Comments about the new stepparent in the household are quite common. This new person is an easy target for a large list of problems, including the divorce itself and discipline of the children.

The child who has been alienated through indoctrination is often quite willing to share his or her opinions and attitudes with other people. For instance, such a child may be taken to a mental health professional for evaluation because of the strong reluctance to visit the other parent. Sometimes it is quite obvious in the interview that the PRP has programmed the child to say specific things to the evaluator. For instance, in the initial meeting with a counselor, a child was asked what the mother had told him to say. The boy responded, "Mommy told me to tell you about all the times that Daddy spanked me with a belt and shut me in a closet." On another occasion, a mother had attempted to give more subtle instructions to her child, who said, "Mommy said not to make Daddy sound any worse than he really is!" Finally, some programmed children sound like little tape recorders. A counselor asked a boy what he had been doing since his last visit. He responded, "I went to the beach with my mother and I played with my mother in the sand and then I played with my Aunt Agnes in the water and I had a very good time." When asked what happened after that, the boy repeated, "I went to the beach with my mother and I played with my mother in the sand and then I played with my Aunt Agnes in the water and I had a very good time."

Sometimes children who have been instructed and programmed to recite criticisms of the NPRP behave in a quite surprising manner when they actually do have time with that parent. There may be some initial resistance, especially when the PRP who did the programming is still in sight, but after a few minutes the child is perfectly happy and cheerful with the NPRP. At the end of the visit, the child may once again become petulant and negativistic when the PRP comes into view. Basically the child is doing her best to be pleasing to both parents.

The process of parental alienation through indoctrination is easy to understand. The process involves an actual culprit who has programmed the child and it is usually easy to hear the words of the parent coming from the mouth of the child. In some situations it is possible to interrupt the process and to help the child be comfortable with both parents. There is another form of parental alienation that is harder to understand. It may be harder to modify once it is in place in the child's mind. For want of a better term, we refer to it as "parental alienation without indoctrination." Another description could be to say that the adversarial process has caused the child to make up his mind to like one parent and dislike the other one.

Parental Alienation Without Indoctrination

The basic issue with this form of parental alienation is that it is hard for a child to maintain affection for two individuals who are persistently and actively fighting with each other. For some children it is not just hard – it is impossible. The result is the child gravitates to either one parent or the other. The child attaches to and identifies with the chosen parent and assumes an attitude of antipathy and hostility to the rejected parent. When this process occurs, the child usually attaches to and identifies with the parent with whom he lives the most, the PRP. That does not seem inevitable, however, since sometimes the child attaches to the missing parent, the NPRP.

We want to emphasize we are referring to situations where the two divorced parents have almost equal merit. That is, they both have been involved with the child-rearing. They both have invested their love, time, energy, and money in their relationships with the child. Although not perfect, they both seem like reasonably nice people and competent parents. We are not talking about situations where it would be completely understandable for the child to firmly love one parent who is nurturing and sober and to firmly despise another parent who is frequently drunk, angry, and abusive. We are not talking about a family where one parent has been a consistent caretaker and the other parent has been absent for many years. In such families it is easy to see why a child might bond with one parent and reject the other. We are referring to family situations where both parents have been available and loving with the child, so it is not obvious why the child bonds with one parent and rejects the other. We are referring to cases such as Annie and Danny at the start of this chapter, in which Danny became firmly attached to his father and firmly rejected his mother's affection.

What makes this happen? How does parental alienation occur when both parents have been reasonable people and indoctrination has not occurred? This is a tragic and common situation and it needs an explanation.

This form of alienation occurs in a way that neither the child himself nor the parents notice. They are too close to the situation to see what is happening. It is important to see that it is almost impossible for a child to love both parents when it is obvious to him the parents are actively, angrily hating each other. The child's mind is not strong enough or sophisticated enough to be able to love Mom (who hates Dad) and also love Dad (who hates Mom). In fact, it is hard enough for adults to handle relationships such as these. If you are friends with a couple who are involved in an extremely angry divorce, you are likely to continue your friendship with one or the other person, but not with both of them. It would be much harder for a small child to remain on friendly, affectionate terms with two parents who are feuding in a major way. In order for the child to accomplish this feat, he would have to say something like this to himself: "I am going to love the part of Mom that loves me, but ignore the part of her that is fighting with Dad; and I'm going to love the part of Dad that loves me, but ignore the part of him that is fighting with Mom." That's a large order for a small child.

The idea that a child might completely reject a parent through this process, without any active indoctrination or intimidation or coercion, is hard for many adults to understand. It is particularly hard for the rejected parent to understand. We will belabor the point with an analogy. A sports fan who lives in Washington, D.C., could easily become an avid and fanatical follower of both the Washington Redskins and the Baltimore Orioles. He could pour an enormous amount of energy and devotion into traveling to games and cheering his favorite football and baseball teams. He would never experience any form of loyalty conflict because the Redskins and the Orioles never compete against each other. On the other hand, is there any way a football fan could be dedicated to both the Redskins and the Dallas Cowboys? Of course not. In fact, any truly loyal Redskins fan would not be neutral about the Cowboys, but would automatically notice and magnify any blemish or defect or failure the Cowboys might show. Likewise, a person who is emotionally involved in a highly adversarial situation is likely to gravitate strongly to one side of the conflict and to reject strongly the other side.

This form of parental alienation is not the result of parental indoctrination or coercion, but is a natural outcome of a highly adversarial relationship between the parents. It is usually not caused by either parent alone, but is created by the battle of both parents together. There may be reasons why the child gravitates to a particular parent. One reason is simply because after the divorce the child lived with one parent more than the other and therefore identified with that parent more closely. In other cases the rejected parent actually did something mean at some time in the past. It may have been a rather minor incident, such as giving the child a spanking. What happens is the child latches onto that small incident and uses it as his explanation for why he despises and avoids that parent. In other words, the sense of alienation of the rejected parent is quite strong, but the child has trouble explaining the depth of his feeling. The child's verbal explanations for the alienation usually seem quite trivial and inadequate. In the short term the child senses it is easier for his emotional well-being to relate to one parent to the exclusion of the other. The long term effects of such decisions can be devastating.

The Continuum of Parental Alienation

In order to explain how parental alienation comes about, this chapter has emphasized the difference between parental alienation which was brought about by indoctrination and parental alienation without indoctrination. It is important to understand the distinction because the question of fault and responsibility may come up. That is, whose fault is it when parental alienation occurs? In the case of parental alienation through indoctrination, the outcome is the fault of the parent who did the brainwashing. In the case of parental alienation without indoctrination, the outcome is not the fault of either parent as an individual. In that circumstance, the alienation was caused by the battle that was fought by both parents, so the child took cover by gravitating completely to one side and away from the other side.

Family relationships are complex and in many cases the parental alienation is not simply the result of one extreme ("with indoctrination") or the other ("without indoctrination"). There is a continuum of cases between these two extremes, in which the alienation is the result of several factors meeting and interacting with each other.

In one case, for example, all three family members, the divorced parents and the 15-year-old daughter, contributed to a severe form of alienation. The girl lived with the mother, but wanted to move to the father's household. After the judge granted her request, the girl was transferred to her father's custody and she never visited her mother again. The girl did not have much explanation for her refusal to visit her mother, other than a few remarks that seemed vague and illogical: "My Mom's hard to live with. My stepfather is overbearing. I never want to see them again." After an evaluation, it seemed that all three of the participants in this drama had important roles. The mother was a rigid, critical person who sometimes was unpleasant company—but her be-havior was certainly not bad enough to justify the daughter's rejection. The father did say a few things to encourage the girl's dislike of the mother—but he did not indoctrinate her or interfere with the visitation. The girl herself contributed to the impasse—she had a narcissistic, self-indulgent personality style and she did not want to inconvenience her-self by maintaining a relationship with her mother. The lesson here is the father, mother, and daughter all contributed to the resulting paren-tal alienation. It did not make sense for any of them to blame the others for what had happened, but they did anyway.

Consider Counseling

A child with parental alienation may be taken to a therapist. First of all, the mother (for instance) will explain to the therapist the child abso-lutely refuses to visit the father. The mother will say she has encour-aged the child to visit many times, but she doesn't want to force the child to visit because he is likely to become hysterical and violent. Al-though the mother claims to want the child to have a good relationship with the father, she understands his reluctance because she knows "the father is a complete bum." When the child is interviewed, he is likely to say basically the same thing as the mother stated, but he is not simply parroting her. In fact, he really believes the father is a bum and he can cite various injustices which occurred several years previously to prove his point. These injustices usually seem rather minor, compared to the total rejection of the father that followed from them.

It is very hard to treat children who manifest parental alienation. Some of these children have firmly made up their minds and it may be difficult to help them understand it is possible to love two parents that may now vigorously battle or hate each other. In therapy, it might be possible to help the child have a good relationship with both parents if the following conditions are met: the parents have finally agreed to a lasting cease fire; both parents really support the notion the child should have a good relationship with both of them; all efforts to indoctrinate, whether blatant or subtle, cease; the child is encouraged, usually by a competent therapist, to spend time with the rejected parent and see what happens; and the child is innately strong enough, brave enough, and flexible enough to reach out to the rejected parent.

In general, the therapist who endeavors to treat the child-victim of parental alienation must be quite active, practical, and somewhat confrontational. In other words, it is not enough for the therapist to sit back and simply ask the child, "Well, how do you feel about your Dad this week?" It does not work to become friends with the child by readily agreeing with the child's misperceptions and, in some cases, lies. The therapist should certainly not support or encourage the child's avoidance of the alienated parent. On the contrary, the therapist should challenge in an appropriate manner the child's mistaken beliefs. The therapist should help the child form new beliefs that are based not on fantasy or hearsay, but on the child's own direct experience with the alienated parent.

It usually takes more than one therapist to deal with a case of parental alienation. Depending on the clinical circumstances, it might work for one therapist to see the child and a separate therapist to be the mediator for the parents. The best way to "treat" parental alienation is to not let it happen in the first place. The next chapter, "Living In Two Homes," gives more suggestions for how to help children have good relationships with both parents.

Chapter Nine
Living in Two Homes

Freddie had a complicated life for a boy in the fourth grade. His parents were divorced—he primarily lived with his mother and had parenting time with his father. His schedule was not unusual for a child in elementary school, in that he stayed with his father every other weekend from Friday afternoon to Sunday evening. His father wanted to maximize their time together, so he arranged to pick Freddie up from school as soon as class ended on Friday afternoon.

Freddie's father had a stubborn streak in him and felt that the mother, the PRP, should be in charge of Freddie's wardrobe. Since he paid child support to the mother, the father did not want to buy any additional clothes for Freddie and did not want to be responsible for washing clothes. The result was that Freddie had to take a small suitcase with him every Friday to school so he would have clothes for the weekend. He and his mother had to make sure he had play clothes for Saturday, church clothes for Sunday, and a couple of clean handkerchiefs. Since those clothes belonged to the mother, she always made sure when Freddie returned on Sunday, all the clothes were returned to her. If one of those handkerchiefs were missing, there was hell to pay.

Although Freddie enjoyed seeing his father, the arrangements set up by his parents became a big headache for him. His weekends with his father always started off badly because it was embarrassing and awkward to take that suitcase to school on those Friday mornings. The time with his father always ended badly because his mom and dad argued when something was missing from the suitcase when he returned home.

Many divorced parents who are working hard to raise their children feel like they are re-inventing the wheel. High schools and colleges do not teach how to raise children when the parents are divorced. It is unlikely that parents would know how to do it from their own past experience, so they end up using trial and error. Chapters Nine through Fourteen give specific suggestions for dealing with common situations that occur when parents are divorced.

Helping the Child To Love Both Parents

Many children of divorced parents actually do have a comfortable, loving relationship with both the mother and the father. These children are lucky. Their parents are not doing anything particularly hard or unusual to bring this about. All they do is refer to the other parent in a neutral or positive tone, rather than with a voice dripping in criticism. They both try to make the time with the NPRP (non-primary residential parent) a positive experience, rather than a recurring dreaded event. If they have a disagreement, they work it out in some way that does not make the child a witness or an unwilling participant. A divorced parent may foster the child's affection for the other parent by helping the child make a simple Christmas present or helping him select an inexpensive card for Mother's Day or Father's Day.

What To Call the Stepparent

One of the things that divorced parents fuss about a lot is what name or term the child uses in referring to a stepparent. In our opinion, parents in both households make too big a deal out of this issue. That is, a man will remarry and will ask his son to refer to the stepmother as "Mommy." The mother, of course, will find out about this and will go through the ceiling. She'll retaliate by insisting the child never refer to the stepmother as "Mommy" in the mother's presence. The poor child may put a lot of energy into working out a system intended to keep everybody happy. In the father's household, he'll call the stepmother "Mommy" and his biological mother "Mom." In the mother's household he'll try to remember to refer to his stepmother as "Bertha" and call his mother "Mommy." Undoubtedly the child will get confused and will sometimes refer to one or another of the adults by the wrong name.

There must be a solution to this common, vexing problem. The solution has two parts. The first part is to help the child find a name or term for the stepparent that he finds natural and comfortable. The child should not be pressured to call the stepparent "Mom" or "Dad" if it makes him feel funny. An informal poll has revealed that most children refer to their stepparents by their given names, such as "George" or "Betty." If

A Lesson From Gandhi

There are many stories about Mahatma Gandhi, who struggled for the independence of India and subsequently tried to reduce the strife between the Muslim and the Hindu peoples of his land. One time a man was very distraught and came to Gandhi for help. The man, who was a Hindu, was in a civil conflict and he killed a Muslim man. The Hindu was sad and upset because the Muslim's son was left an orphan. He asked Gandhi for forgiveness. Gandhi suggested the Hindu adopt the child, which the man agreed to do. Then Gandhi added that the Hindu man should devote his life to raising the boy to be a devout Muslim. It must evoke a similar feeling, when divorced parents are asked to help their children have a healthy and affectionate relationship with their former spouses.

given permission to use the stepparent's first name, the child rapidly gets comfortable with it. Also, it makes it much easier to know whom he is talking about.

The second part to the solution is to be completely tolerant when the child later gets the names mixed up and uses the wrong one. Every so often the child is going to refer to his mother as "Betty" or his stepmother as "Mommy." Don't make it into a big deal. The child will usually correct himself and continue on with the conversation. Names are not important, especially to the child. Statistically both ex-spouses will remarry—all the adults involved should treat the new spouse with respect. It is a wonderful lesson for the child.

Continuity in Activities

There are many simple, practical things parents can do to help children adjust to living in two households. To start with, it might help for the adult to put himself or herself in the child's place. For most adults, it would be really aggravating if every few days they had to change their phone number, their bed, their wardrobe, and their entire family. With a little extra effort, divorced parents can minimize the daily and weekly disruptions their children experience.

Parents should figure out a way for their children to maintain friendships, extracurricular activities, and special interests, regardless of which household the child happens to be in. To be specific, it should be possible for a youngster to be on a soccer team and get to the practices and the games, no matter which parent he happens to be with at the time. It should be possible for the child to attend a classmate's birthday party, even if he is with the NPRP that weekend. It should be possible for the child to be active in the Boy Scouts, even if he is living with the NPRP every other weekend. In fact, it might be a good idea for the NPRP to volunteer as the assistant to the soccer coach or one of the leaders for the Tiger Cubs, since this would help the parent and the child have a regular activity together.

Spending the Night

A popular activity for children is spending the night with a friend. For some reason, NPRPs have the idea children should never spend the night with a friend on the weekend when the child is staying in the non-primary residence. Sometimes the NPRP has the idea his parenting time should mean he and the child are together and nobody else is around. It would seem more natural for the NPRP and the child to try to enter each other's schedules, rather than trying to design "quality time" together.

For instance, suppose your child wants to have a friend sleep over on Saturday night, when he is at the NPRP's household. Most child visitors don't need much space—they usually bring their own sleeping bags. The NPRP might even want to include the visiting child's parents for a casual Saturday evening dinner or a simple Sunday morning brunch. The main point is that these are ways for the NPRP to enter his child's world and to have a greater involvement in the child's day-to-day life. The purpose of parenting time is to fulfill the child's needs, not the parent's. The needs of these children can be addressed in a more effective manner if the NPRP also develops relationships with the child's friends.

Clothes and Toys

Is there some way children like Freddie, who was mentioned at the beginning of this chapter, would not have to take a suitcase with him to school every Friday? The simplest solution would be for him to have a supply of everyday clothes in both of his homes. He should also have a supply of games, toys, and books in both homes. Ideally, a younger child would even have a Teddy bear or a special blanket in both homes. The way to make that happen is allow the child to develop an attachment to two special blankets at the same time. At some point the child leaves one of the blankets at the home of the NPRP, so the child ends up with a transitional object in both places. By the way, some therapists will say this can't be done. They learned about the importance of transitional objects in graduate school and they have assumed children can be attached to only one special object at a time. In some ways, however, children are more adaptable than we give them credit.

What about presents? We think there should be some coordination between divorced parents regarding major presents, such as expensive bicycles, watches, ski equipment, and so on. In many cases, the parent may want to select a present related to an activity the parent and child enjoy together. Some divorced parents have major battles over whether a child will take a particular present with him to the other household. We think the child should have personal possessions in both homes and it generally works best if he leaves presents in the household where he received them. So the PRP will give the child a few Christmas presents, which stay in that home; the NPRP will give the child a few presents, which will stay in that home.

However, we don't think parents should always insist that presents should stay in their respective homes. If you give your son a watch for his birthday, you should let him wear it to the other household—and you should accept the possibility he may lose it there! Parents should be more concerned with the well-being of the child rather than what makes Mom or Dad happy. Once again, common sense and communication are key.

Coordinating Discipline

Children and adolescents in intact homes are skillful at getting their way by manipulating their parents. Children seem to take a course in kindergarten on how to identify the parent who is most likely to grant them a particular favor. When parents are divorced, manipulative children have a field day. Not only do the parents not communicate, but the parents and other relatives may feel sorry for the child and may be overly indulgent.

Many children are not consciously trying to work the parents against each other, but are merely trying to have their own needs met. Other children knowingly take advantage of their parents' divorce in order to achieve their own purposes. For example, a 15-year-old girl explained

---

Coordinating Parenting Through the Internet

It is not surprising that enterprising divorced parents have found a way to share family information, communicate regarding events and activities, and coordinate parenting time schedules through an Internet website. If you are interested in this approach, check out OurFamilyWizard.com. This website was developed by two divorced parents after conferring with family law attorneys, mediators, and parenting consultants.

On Our Family Wizard, each family has their own section that can only be accessed by themselves. The children can access the parts that pertain to them. The website contains the current schedule for the children, but just about everything else that both parents need to know: vital statistics; emergency contact numbers; insurance cards; names of doctors and dentists; health history; child care providers; school information; and even an expense log by various categories. Schedules can easily be printed out and posted on the refrigerator. Instead of using e-mail, important family messages can be posted on the family's digital bulletin board. All of this information can be accessed from any computer or BlackBerry. This seems like a clever way to help divorced parents communicate more effectively and—as a result—have less to argue about.

---

eloquently and somewhat remorsefully how she used her parents' divorce for her own advantage. She knew if she actively stirred up trouble between her parents, they would not be talking with each other and would not check out her stories with each other. She could then claim her mother had given her permission to do something in order to influence her father, and vice versa.

Most children find life is less confusing if the basic rules are consistent. Although divorced parents are not expected to agree on every aspect of raising their children, it is helpful if they coordinate the most common decisions that arise almost every day. For example: "Bedtime is 9 p.m. on school nights and 10 p.m. on weekends." "You may go to PG-13 movies, but no R-rated movies." "You had D's on your report card, so you cannot use the car until the next report card." When it comes to discipline, the last thing Parent A should do is befriend the child by letting him get away with something Parent B does not allow.

Of course, life is not perfect and even parents in intact families may disagree on discipline and be inconsistent. We are simply suggesting it is in the child's interests if divorced parents were to make some attempt at agreeing on the most common household rules. Children need rules. Having different standards in different households is both confusing and harmful.

Enjoying the Usual Routine

Sometimes NPRPs feel they need to be superparents during every moment of their visitation or parenting time. They entertain their children intensively and plan extraordinary activities for each weekend they have together. We doubt they have much fun. Parenting means more than participating in playtime. Through assistance in the day-to-day development of the child, parents can be the role models they should be.

It probably makes more sense to have a regular, rather predictable routine during visitation, such as: cooking a meal together; doing some errands or some chores together; doing something fun together, but it does not have to be anything elaborate. It sometimes works well for the parent and child to develop or expand on a common hobby or interest. It could be a hobby like photography or collecting bugs, which has a visible, tangible product. Or it could be an activity like hiking or tennis, that the child and parent enjoy doing together. In either case, the child and the NPRP develop a sense of continuity by working on the same project or activity from week to week. When this process works, the child looks forward to the next visitation. There is more on the subject of visitation in the next chapter.

Chapter Ten
Making Parenting Time Work

Maggie Folsom, age 9, lived primarily with her mother and had parenting time with her father every other weekend and every Wednesday evening. Her mother was a nervous woman who was very concerned about Maggie and wanted to assure herself that Maggie was not having any problems when she was at her father's house. Therefore, Ms. Folsom started to telephone Maggie every weekend on Saturday morning, Saturday evening, and Sunday morning. These phone calls interrupted Maggie's activities, so the girl became abrupt and sounded irritated with her mother. Maggie tried to avoid the phone calls and made them as brief as she could. Ms. Folsom thought that Maggie was not acting like her usual self on the telephone, so she started worrying even more and questioned the girl in detail when she returned from the father's household. Since the phone calls and the interrogations made the father's parenting time unpleasant for Maggie, she started to say she would rather not visit her father so frequently. Ms. Folsom became convinced the father was neglecting or even abusing Maggie, so she petitioned the court to curtail his parenting time.

Divorced parents put an enormous amount of energy into fussing and fuming about the child's schedule and activities in the other parent's household. Just for starters, almost every PRP (primary residential parent) will be concerned that the NPRP's (non-primary residential parent's) parenting times interfere with or seriously compromise the child's usual activities. For instance, "Jimmy will be severely traumatized because he will be visiting his father in Cleveland instead of having ice cream at his best friend's birthday party." Almost every NPRP will believe that the child's emotional, social, and educational problems would be solved if only his or her parenting times were longer and more frequent. Children feel miserable when their parents argue about their schedule; about whether the child is ready on time, which is blamed on the PRP; about whether the child gets back on time, which is blamed on the NPRP; and what actually happened during the time with the other parent.

Typical Schedules for NPRP Parenting Time

It is possible to state some general guidelines regarding parenting time schedules that are related to the age of the child. Because of individual differences and special family circumstances, however, there are many reasons why divorced parents might work out a schedule that differs from these guidelines. These suggestions are meant to be a starting point for more detailed discussions.

Very Young Children

There may be some difference of opinion about what is the best living arrangement for very young children, up to age 2. Some professionals say very young children need almost complete stability and need to sleep in the same bed in the same home every night. Others say very young children can easily handle multiple caretakers and certain kinds of change in their daily routine. There are thousands of young children in day care—these children spend about half of their waking hours during the course of the week at the day care center and about half at home. With that in mind, wouldn't those same children be able to handle living about half the time with the mother and about half the time with the father?

Suppose the divorced couple agreed the mother were to work and the father were to stay home for two years. The child could live with the father during the days and half of each weekend; the child could live with the mother every evening and the other half of each weekend. We think most people would agree—if the mother were working full-time—it would be better for the child to stay with the father during the days than to be placed in a day care center. The reverse arrangement would also apply, if the father worked and the mother stayed home for two years. In these circumstances, the child could live with the mother during the days and half of each weekend; the child could live with the father every evening and the other half of each weekend.

Suppose both parents worked and the divorced couple hired a babysitter. The child could live in the mother's home for one week, with the babysitter supervising her during the day. The child could live with the father the next week, with the same babysitter during the days. The child would have the continuity of the babysitter and also have a relationship with both parents. These arrangements may seem unusual to some people, but they appear to work. The main point is a young child can form attachments to several people (mother, father, babysitter, grandmother) and be comfortable with any of them.

If the young child, up to age 2, is already quite comfortable with both mother and father, parenting time could have practically any schedule. The arrangement could even be living half the time with each parent. The child should continue to be comfortable with both parents if both the PRP and the NPRP see the child frequently and regularly.

What if the young child is not familiar with or comfortable with the NPRP? Here, the goal of the parenting time is for the child to become attached to the NPRP, so they will be comfortable with each other. In general, they should start with brief episodes of parenting time, usually in the PRP's household, and then gradually increasing the child's exposure to the NPRP. The NPRP's parenting times should be brief, but frequent. For example, they may be several times a week for two hours at a time. During those times the NPRP should actually be in charge of the child, like a babysitter or a nanny. He would be there to feed the child, change the diapers, and perhaps put the child down for a nap, if that were the child's routine at the end of the visitation time.

Since the NPRP's parenting time with young children frequently takes place in the PRP's home, the question will arise as to what the PRP should do during that time. It would be best if she could keep out of the way, so the child and the NPRP could really feel like they are spending time together. If there has been a lot of conflict between the parents, it would be nice if the mother could be out of the home during the time of the father's parenting time. Although it might be hard to make the arrangements, since it would mean having a neutral person stay in the home with the NPRP, keeping the two parents away from each other might save wear and tear on everybody. Even as an infant, hostility can be sensed.

Preschool children

Children who are age 2 to 5 usually live primarily in one household and have parenting time in the home of the NPRP. Although there is no exact formula for what the parenting time should be, a typical schedule might provide for two visits a week. For example, a 4-year-old might be with the NPRP every other weekend with one overnight, such as Saturday morning to Sunday afternoon. In addition, the child might be with the NPRP on one or two weekday evenings each week. To provide a

---

Developmental Tasks

There are specific developmental tasks children ordinarily accomplish in a step-by-step fashion as they get older. For example, there are physical tasks such as learning to sit up, crawl, walk, and run. There are also psychological tasks and these tasks should be considered in devising visitation arrangements for children of different ages.

The psychological task for *very young children* (up to age 2) is to develop a sense of trust in their primary caretakers.

The psychological task for *toddlers* (about age 2 to 4) is the process of separation and individuation. This means the child has a sense of his own individuality and he becomes comfortable with brief separations from primary caretakers.

The task for *preschoolers* (about age 4 to 6) is to define themselves within the family, which usually takes the form of identifying with traits in the parents.

The task for *school children* (about age 6 to 12) is to achieve a sense of self-worth through mastery of skills.

The task for *adolescents* (about age 13 to 18) is to establish an identity separate from the parents.

---

second example following the same principle, the parenting time of the NPRP could be every Tuesday evening for dinner and one overnight every weekend, from Friday evening to Saturday evening. Schedules should focus on helping children maintain a positive relationship with both parents.

School Age Children

As children get older, the parenting time with the NPRP is usually less frequent but longer in duration. For example, older children might be with the NPRP every other weekend with two overnights, such as Friday evening to Sunday evening. In addition, they might be with the NPRP on one weekday evening each week. There is no rule that the parenting time must follow this schedule, since it might be convenient to do it differently. For instance, there may be an advantage for some divorced parents to arrange for the NPRP's parenting time to occur every weekend, from Saturday morning to Sunday evening, in order to have the child on a regular weekly schedule.

Adolescents

When children enter high school, the schedule for parenting times becomes more individualized. Many youngsters continue to be with the NPRP every other weekend, but the actual schedule becomes more variable because other activities are occurring in their lives. By this time the weekday evening parenting times with the NPRP have usually ended.

In the stressful time following the divorce, it is helpful to have a definite parenting time schedule that has been planned out months ahead of time. It usually works best for both parents to adhere to the schedule religiously. The reason for the strict schedule is that it gives the newly divorced parents one less thing to argue about. It is extremely reassuring to the child to know she will be seeing the NPRP at a regular, predictable time each week. Once the dust settles, it might not be so necessary to stick to such a rigid schedule. It may be a sign the divorced parents are getting more comfortable working out issues with each other when they mutually agree to deviate from the schedule already planned out. These years are critical in child development. Parents must work together during these years in order to prevent many dangerous situations.

Siblings

There is a tendency in these cases for parents, attorneys, judges, and therapists to invent or develop very strict, rigid rules they feel should be followed by all divorced families. One of the "rules" we have heard several times is that all of the siblings should have the exact same parenting time schedule. The judge may say, for instance, the four minor children (ages 16, 10, 8, and 2) will primarily live with the mother and will have parenting time with the father every other weekend. The judge literally means all four children will visit the father, *en masse,* on every occasion the father's parenting time occurs. To us, such an arrangement does not make any sense at all.

When there are several children, parenting time should be scheduled in a way that maximizes the ability of the NPRP to spend meaningful time with each child. If the children had different parenting time schedules, the result would be that *both* parents would be able to spend time with the children individually. In the family with the four children, suppose the 16-year-old is a girl. Since her weekends are busy, she and her father agree they will have dinner together every Wednesday evening. Let's suppose the 10-year-old and 8-year-old children are boys. The parents agree the boys will have parenting time with the father together every other weekend, Friday evening to Sunday evening. And the 2-year-old is a little girl. The dad sees her every Tuesday evening and every other weekend, Friday evening to Saturday afternoon. The younger girl and the two boys alternate, so that one weekend the father has the daughter and the next weekend he has the two boys together.

This father would need to keep his calendar organized, since he has parenting time with one or two of his children most of the days of every week. This not only helps him be a better parent but will also be a benefit to the other parent. The reader should not go overboard and become rigid in the opposite direction. We are not suggesting the four children in the example *never* have parenting time with the father together. There hopefully will be some occasions—for instance, a special picnic, a week of summer vacation—when the father and the four children would be together at the same time.

Transition Times

The most difficult time for young children is the transition from one household to another. It is disruptive; it means separation from a loving parent; it means an interruption in the day's activities; it means some inevitable tension, as the child's care is being passed from one parent to the other. The last thing the child needs is to witness hostility, sarcasm, and resentment.

Some parents, who get on each other's nerves, structure the transition in such a way that the parents do not have to speak to each other. For instance, if the mother is picking the child up from the father's home, it is agreed the mother will stay in her car and the father will stay on the porch, while the child walks out to the car to leave. What kind of example is that for our children? Is it beneficial for them to see two people who at one time showed enough love to have a child now cannot even be civil to each other? This is not the best way to design the transition from one household to the other.

Perhaps a better way to avoid parental conflict at the transition times is to arrange it so both parents are not present when the transition occurs. For example, if a young child is in day care, it might work smoothly for the father to pick the child up for weekend parenting time on Friday afternoon and return the child to the day care program on Monday morning.

If the transitions are not occurring smoothly, the parents may need to meet with a counselor or mediator to work out a pleasant way for the child to go from one household to the other. In extreme cases, the transition may occur at the therapist's office. For instance, suppose there has been a great deal of conflict between the parents and the child has been caught up in it, so the entire divorced family is in counseling. The counselor could schedule the appointments for Friday afternoons. The mother brings the child to the appointment and the counselor spends the first part of the meeting with the mother and child together, reviewing the plans for the father's parenting time. Then the mother leaves. A little while later the father arrives and the latter part of the therapy meeting is with the father and child together, in which they review again the plans for the weekend. At the end of the session, the child leaves with the father.

In some communities there are organizations or agencies that assist divorced parents who are not able to find a way for their children to move peaceably from one household to the other. These organizations provide a place where transitions can occur calmly and safely. This program is provided by the Exchange Club in some communities, which is a national service organization. In some areas, the Court Appointed Special Advocates (CASAs), Catholic Charities, and other organizations sponsor programs that serve the same purpose. Some of these programs also make it possible for the NPRP to have supervised parenting time for a modest fee, if ordered by a court. Sadly, some of these exchanges take place at police departments. Is this not a terrible example for our children?

Consideration for the Child's Wishes

Divorced parents sometimes go to unusual extremes with their children. Some parents become overly indulgent. Others have a rejecting attitude toward the child, because they have transferred feelings from the ex-spouse to the child. Divorced parents may have a hard time figuring out how much to consider the child's preferences and demands, especially regarding the parenting time schedule. In many situations it is helpful for the parents to think through whether it is best for the child to have very much say about the schedule, before making the actual decision.

Parents can err by giving too much consideration to the child's stated preferences. For example, the PRP may announce the child can see the other parent whenever he wants. Or she may ask the child if he wants to be with the father this weekend or if he wants to stay at the mother's home. This may seem like the mother is trying to be helpful to the child, but actually she is making it hard on him. Giving the child control over his schedule tends to put the child in the middle and intensifies his loyalty conflicts, because it is forcing the child to choose whether he wants to be with Mommy or Daddy.

Some parents simply don't see when they believe they are doing something nice for the child, they are actually putting him in a meat grinder. Another time a parent may be tempted to give the child's opinion too much consideration is when the child calls up and wants to be taken home. Ordinarily it is better for the child to continue the parenting time with the NPRP until the end of the scheduled time. Do we as parents let children decide when they want to go to school? Isn't the relationship with the other parent just as important as the child's education?

Parents can err by giving too little consideration to the child's preferences. Parents should listen to the child's point of view, since they may get some good ideas. An example of giving too little consideration was the case of Merrie and Melodie at the beginning of Chapter Seven. In that case the two parents had agreed on joint legal and physical custody and arranged for their teenage daughters to alternate between the two households, one week at a time. The children simply wanted to live in one place and visit the other parent. The parents had been pretending to do what was in the best interests of the children, to have continuing relationships with both of them, but were actually putting their own career needs above the children.

A general principle is parents should give more consideration to the child's opinions and wishes as the child gets older. With younger children, it ordinarily works best for the adults to listen to the child's opinions, for the adults to make the decision, and then to stick to it. With older children and adolescents, it works better to have a greater amount of discussion and negotiation. The other parent should obviously be included in these decisions.

Giving Up Control

In divorced families, parents should expect everyday events will not always go smoothly. As a result, no parent is going to be able to be in total control all the time. Parents have to give up the notion the children are always going to be happy and comfortable. Growing up with divorced parents involves a certain amount of unhappiness and there is no way to avoid it.

Giving up control means the NPRP will need to accept that the PRP will be making most of the decisions, especially those involving education and medical care and most day-to-day discipline.

Giving up control means the PRP will not have complete knowledge or complete authority when the child is in the other parent's household. During this time the NPRP will need to be responsible for the child's recreational activities, for her dinner, and for necessary medical care. In particular, parents like Ms. Folsom, at the beginning of this chapter, will need to let the child have her time with the father without repeatedly intruding.

Some parents may be a little anxious when the children are away for the weekend, but they need to learn patience and resolve the anxiety within themselves. These anxious parents benefit the children when they refrain from making overly frequent phone calls. If they don't hear from their PRPs every single day, these children are more likely to feel stronger and able to be more emotionally self-sufficient. Encouraging the children to minimize the phone calls gives them the opportunity to develop other family bonds. This helps the children become more well-rounded and independent.

Chapter Eleven
Holidays and Holy Days

Mr. Holmes called his attorney on a Thursday afternoon in a complete tizzy. It had dawned on him the following Sunday, only three days away, was Father's Day. Although he had visitation with the children every other weekend, they were not scheduled to be with him that particular Sunday. He felt greatly aggrieved because he remembered the visitation schedule had resulted in the children spending Mother's Day with their mother. Mr. Holmes called his attorney, who called the mother's attorney, who called the mother, who said, "I'm terribly sorry, but the children and I had already made plans to go on a picnic on Sunday afternoon with family friends, so they will not be able to see their father that day." The mother's attorney called the father's attorney, who called the father and said, "Too bad, but your ex-wife stubbornly refuses to let the children be with you on Father's Day." Mr. Holmes felt himself becoming furious and indignant. He went home early, skipped dinner, and put away four double Scotch and waters.

Divorced parents and the judges who tell them how to organize their lives have found many different ways to deal with holidays and other special occasions. Sometimes the divorce decrees have very elaborate schedules designating how the holidays will be spent for years to come. Most judges have the idea the way to make important holidays equal for the two parents is to alternate them from year to year. In other words, the judge might say this year the children will be with the father on Thanksgiving during the day until 4 p.m. and with the mother from 4 until 9 p.m.; with the father on Christmas Eve until 8 a.m. on Christmas Day, and then spend the rest of the day with the mother. The next year will be the reverse of this year: the children will be with the mother on Thanksgiving during the day until 4 p.m. and with the father from 4 until 9 p.m.; with the mother on Christmas Eve until 8 a.m. on Christmas Day, and then spend the rest of the day with the father.

Parents and judges sometimes make detailed provisions for particular days that seem rather minor on the scale of events, such as Mother's Day, Father's Day, and each parent's birthday. In fact, some of these special occasions never received more that a fleeting notice by either the children or the parents until the divorce negotiations got under way.

Another common error is the notion the children should fully celebrate every important occasion with both of the divorced parents every year. It is not unusual, for instance, for children of divorced parents to be subjected to two complete Thanksgiving dinners; to be entertained by Santa in all his regalia in both households; and to celebrate each of his birthdays twice, complete with duplicate parties.

Self-Centered Parents

What is wrong with these complicated schedules and duplicated celebrations? The most important thing wrong with them is the parents, who devise them, are working from an egocentric and perhaps a selfish point of view. The parent seems to be saying to herself, "It is really important for my child to celebrate Thanksgiving with me and my relatives this year." The other parent is, of course, saying the same thing to himself, but neither one of them is correct. The parent doesn't realize she is really defining what is important to herself, that is, the child be with her on this special day. What actually is important to the child is to enjoy a day like Thanksgiving with one of his parents and perhaps with the parent's extended family or close friends. If it goes well, the child is going to feel about as thankful as he can. Trying to squeeze in two Thanksgiving celebrations with two different families is simply going to make him feel rushed, used by both parents, and stuffed.

The people who devise the complicated schedules that alternate from year to year have the idea it is important for the children of divorced parents to participate in the traditions of both the mother's household and the father's household. That certainly sounds right, and we are not disagreeing with this basic premise. However, the judges and the attorneys who make up the schedules seem to have a very superficial notion as to how family traditions actually play themselves out. They seem to know family traditions are going to be important for these children, even though their parents are divorced, but then they create schedules which are surely going to prevent the children from ever fully experiencing a true family tradition.

Importance of Tradition

What is a family tradition and why does it even matter? Most of the significant family traditions involve the merging of three components:

• A specific event or day, such as: Rosh Hashanah, Christmas, a wedding, the last two weeks of August at the beach
• A particular group of people: close family, friends, neighbors, grandparents, other extended family
• An activity that involves family or community values: the religious implications of Hanukkah and Christmas, the patriotic aspect of a parade on the Fourth of July, the romantic aspect of a wedding.

This is the prescription, which is fairly simple, for creating and perpetuating family traditions. A child who grows up in an intact family in which traditions are consistently observed starts to blend together the feelings that are associated with the event, the people involved, and the values. If the occasions are reasonably pleasant and happy, the child would be more likely to assimilate the values that are associated with the event.

For the child to benefit from family traditions, however, the experience must be administered in a consistent manner, on a regular schedule, and in the right dose. Ideally, the child would have the same basic experience with the same set of important people (relatives and close family friends) year after year. We doubt that a child, whose parents are divorced, would incorporate anything very useful from holidays marked by hustling from one household to another, arguments over the exact schedule for the day, and cursory contacts with both sets of grandparents. The challenge for divorced parents is to find a way to help the children experience a strong sense of family tradition, even though they are growing up in two different households.

Dividing the Holidays and Holy Days

We have a specific suggestion for how divorced parents should deal with holidays. Our approach is intended to maximize the children's sense of being truly involved in family traditions rather than being part-time players in other people's special days. What we recommend is that the parents make a list of all the holidays and holy days they consider meaningful. Then they divide up the days in an equitable manner. The division that is established would continue indefinitely. In other words: (1) the child would only be in one household for any particular special day and (2) the child will be in the same household for that day every year.

For instance, two divorcing parents made this list of the days that they considered meaningful:

> Christmas Eve
> Christmas Day
> Thanksgiving Day
> Friday after Thanksgiving
> Memorial Day weekend
> Labor Day weekend
> New Year's Day
> Fourth of July

In this system it usually works out best to divide up the really big occasions into two parts, such as: Christmas Eve and Christmas Day; Thanksgiving Day and the Friday after Thanksgiving. Since there were eight meaningful days for these parents, they divided them up so that each parent had four. The father ended up with Christmas Eve, Thanksgiving Day, New Year's Day, and Memorial Day weekend. The father will always have the children on Christmas Eve, year in and year out. It means he can construct his own consistent tradition for his children for that day. The children will grow up feeling Christmas Eve has a warm, consistent, and predictable feeling to it. In this particular case the mother ended up with Christmas Day; the Friday after Thanksgiving; the Fourth of July; and Labor Day weekend. She will feel good because she and her children will develop a consistent and predictable way to celebrate Christmas. The mother and the children will always be able to attend her family's traditional picnic on the Fourth of July. Her children will grow up feeling they are an important part of that Fourth of July picnic because they are there every single year.

The actual process of dividing the days is simply taking turns. Somebody flips a coin to see which parent goes first, and then they alternate choosing days. If the parents are able to talk to each other without serious arguing, they can achieve a good result by conversation and negotiation. This method of dividing the holidays works well when the list consists of about eight or ten special days during the year. This method does not work well if it is pushed to include more and more days, because it begins to disrupt the basic parenting time schedule that should be predictable for the children.

Mother's Day, Father's Day

There may be many special days that deserve some degree of recognition, but do not really need to be celebrated exactly on the right date. We would put Mother's Day, Father's Day, and the parents' own birthdays in this category. For instance, we think it is a good idea for the child to recognize Father's Day and his father's birthday with a card, a small present the child made himself, and perhaps a phone call if he happens to be in his mother's household that day. But it does not need to be much more than that and the child does not actually need to be with the father on that particular day. Days are not special just because they are called a special day. Days are special when a parent gets to spend time with his or her child.

In an intact home, the celebration of the father's birthday and Father's Day is usually instigated by the mother, not the children. In a divorced family, the mother will usually need to remind a young child that Father's Day is coming up and the mother might even need to help the child prepare a card for her former husband. (The father should make the same effort for his ex-spouse.) When we make this suggestion—that the mother remind the child and help him honor the dad on Father's Day—we sense the collective jaw dropping of some readers. We realize some parents are so hateful of each other that promoting the child's affection for the other parent is the last thing they could imagine. But this is exactly what we have in mind, that it is the responsibility of both of the parents to help the children have a strong, positive attachment to both of the parents.

Some divorcing couples may feel strongly Mother's Day and Father's Day and perhaps other days should be considered important enough to be on the list of special days to be officially divided. That's fine, since different families have their own interests and values. In general, however, divorced parents should try to agree on using holidays to create a sense of family tradition for the children. What this means is parents should try to think about the meaning of the holiday and the actual experience of the day from the child's point of view, and not simply to consider their own priorities.

Religious Wars

If the divorced parents are active in different religions, it is possible the list of holidays and holy days will be quite diverse. The list may include some combination of Christmas Eve, Christmas Day, Holy Thursday, Good Friday, Easter, Diwali, Pongal, Kwanzaa, Ramadan, Day of Arafat, Rosh Hashanah, Yom Kippur, Sukkot, Hanukkah, Passover, and Summer Solstice. Perhaps the mother is Presbyterian, so she wants to have the children on Christmas Day and Easter. The father is Muslim, so he chooses to have the children during significant parts of the month of Ramadan and the Day of Arafat. We realize it may be confusing to young children to be exposed to two contradictory religious traditions. Probably it would be preferable for the parents to agree on raising young children in only one religion, and allowing them to learn about the other parent's religion when they are older.

Many courts have addressed this topic, as to how to raise the children when the parents have extremely different opinions about religion. In some cases, such as *Zummo vs. Zummo* (574 A.2d 1130), the decisions were appealed to higher courts and the opinions were published. This case also illustrates how different courts reach different conclusions on this touchy issue.

It is sad when strongly religious parents have major misunderstandings and angry confrontations over the children's observance of holy days. Suppose, for example, a Jewish man married a Baptist woman and they had two children. Since the father was intensely religious, the couple agreed the children would be raised as Jews. When the parents divorced, the mother readily agreed the children would continue to attend Hebrew school every weekend, regardless of whether the children were residing at the father's home or the mother's home. This arrangement continued peaceably until the mother remarried—and the new stepfather was a staunch Southern Baptist. The stepfather was also deeply religious and he was sincerely concerned the children would go to hell unless they were baptized and born again. Because of the stepfather's influence, the mother started taking the children to a Baptist Sunday school rather than to Hebrew school on her weekends. What bothered the biological father most was that she started telling the children they were "half Jewish and half Christian." There were serious arguments, of course, over how to celebrate Hanukkah/Christmas and Passover/Easter.

Important Case: *Zummo vs. Zummo* (574 A.2d 1130)

Before Pamela Zummo and David Zummo married in 1978, they discussed their religious differences—Pamela was Jewish and David was raised Roman Catholic. They agreed to raise their children in the Jewish faith and during their marriage, the Zummo family participated fully in the life of the Jewish community. They celebrated Sabbath every Friday night and attended all of the High Holiday services as well.

When they divorced, Pamela was awarded primary physical custody of the three children while David was given visitation that included every other weekend. During David's weekends, he refused to arrange for their son's attendance at the Jewish Sunday school and he wished to take his children to occasional Catholic services. Pamela opposed exposing the children to a second religion that would confuse and disorient them.

The trial court supported the mother's position. The court stated the father was obligated to take the children to their synagogue's Sunday school and he was not permitted to take the children to religious services contrary to the Jewish faith. The trial court concluded that restrictions upon the father's right to expose his children to his religious beliefs were permissible and appropriate.

In 1989 David Zummo appealed this case to the Superior Court of Pennsylvania, asserting his constitutional rights and those of his children had been violated by the order. The Superior Court held that: (1) the oral prenuptial agreement regarding the religious upbringing of the children was not enforceable; (2) an order prohibiting a father from taking his children to religious services contrary to the Jewish faith during lawful periods of visitation did violate his constitutional rights. The Superior Court reversed the ruling of the lower court on these decisions. However, the Superior Court did affirm the decision that the father present his children at Synagogue for Sunday school during his periods of weekend visitation.

In situations like this—the Jewish dad and the Baptist mom—it is unlikely the parents would be able to work out an agreement between themselves once they have become entrenched in their respective foxholes. When the parents are immovable, even a skillful mediator may not be able to help them reach a compromise. Cases like this often end up in court and the judge is expected to resolve the dispute or at least settle it. We suggest the judge think along the following lines:

- In general, each parent has the right to take the children to the parent's choice of religious activity. With this in mind, the mother can take the children to Baptist events.
- However, the mother previously agreed the children would be raised Jewish, so the mother should allow the father to take the children to Hebrew school every Sunday during the school year. The mother's loss of parenting time would be made up elsewhere in the weekly schedule.
- It is very confusing for children to hear their parents contradict each other, as when the father said, "You're Jewish!" and the mother said, "You're half Jewish and half Christian!" Since the mother previously agreed the children would be raised Jewish, she may not tell the children they are "half Christian."
- Neither the mother, the stepfather, nor anybody else should tell the children they are going to hell unless they are baptized.
- When the children are older (that is, adolescents), they can learn about other religions and decide for themselves what they prefer.

Special Days and Parenting Plans

Parenting plans were discussed in detail in Chapter Six. The allocations of holidays and holy days is an excellent example of how useful it is to put the time and energy up front into a detailed parenting plan. Even before the divorce occurs, the parents can sit down and specify how the most significant holidays will be observed for the duration of the agreement. We think it works best to divide the special days between the parents and stick to the same schedule year after year. If the process works, we hope there will be at least three payoffs. First, there will be less bickering each year over the details of how to spend the holidays, since the children and the parents get used to the schedule stated in the parenting plan. Secondly, there is greater opportunity for the children to experience family and community traditions because they engage in the same activities each year. And third, it is less likely that unexpected events (such as the mother marrying the Southern Baptist) will cause misunderstanding and arguing, because it is clear what the parents agreed to in the original parenting plan.

Chapter Twelve
Moving Near and Far

Roger grew up in a suburb of Washington, D.C., in Northern Virginia. Although his parents divorced when he was a small child, they managed to communicate in a constructive manner and coordinate their parenting activities. Roger's mother was the custodial parent, but Roger's father was actively involved in his son's school and recreational activities. For instance, the father was the assistant coach for Roger's soccer team.

Both of Roger's parents remarried. When Roger was 13 and about to start the 8th grade, his stepfather was offered a career-enhancing job in Colorado. Roger was both excited and distraught—he was excited about the prospect of living in an area where everybody learned to ride a horse, but he resented that his mother and stepfather would separate him from his many friends and teammates in Virginia. With as much maturity as he could muster, Roger told both of his parents about his concerns. In fact, Roger made the proposal that he live with his father in Virginia during the school year and with his mother in Colorado during most of his vacations.

Since Roger's parents had a long history of healthy communication and successful co-parenting, it was fairly easy for them to agree to Roger's proposal and work out the details. For example, Roger's mother visited Roger (and some of her old friends) in Northern Virginia several weekends out of the year. Roger traveled to Colorado during parts of his Christmas vacations, spring vacations, and summer vacations. During the summers he arranged for one or another friend to go with him to Colorado, and they learned how to ride horses together. Children of divorce frequently suffer when one of their parents moves a long distance away, but Roger was a youngster who found a way to make it work to his advantage. Fortunately, he had a reasonable mother and father who both wanted Roger to have a good relationship with both of his parents.

Our society today is obviously a mobile one with approximately one in five Americans changing residence each year. Relocations are often necessary because of changes in employment, education, career opportunities, and—in cases of divorce—remarriage to another spouse. It is unrealistic to imagine that divorced parents will always live in the same community after their divorce, but it is a goal for which every divorced parent should strive. It is unfair to constantly uproot children whose family life has already been modified by a divorce. It is unwise for a primary residential parent (PRP) to take the children far away from the non-primary residential parent (NPRP) with only occasional parenting time due to time and money constraints, since it will undoubtedly cause the children to grow up without equal participation from both parents. Courts have struggled with this issue for a number of years and taking this factor into account is just one of the considerations in determining what is in the long-term, best interests of the children.

Nationwide, courts usually consider four factors in determining whether changing a child's residence to a distant location is in a child's best interest. These factors include the following:

• The respective advantages of the move in improving the PRP's and the child's quality of life.
• The integrity of the PRP's motive for relocation.
• The integrity of the NPRP's reasons for opposing the move.
• The potential negative impact of the move on the relationship between the NPRP and the child.

The decision to relocate will hopefully be made after a frank discussion between the parents of the children involved. Parents who are truly focused on the long-term welfare of the children should work together to address any relocation issues. In the event the matter still goes to court, the development of evidence is critical. For example, parents opposing relocation should demonstrate the child's very strong attachment to the original location by evaluating the amount of time the child resided in the community, the time spent with family and friends providing third party support, and the school history.

A long, successful history in a community is important. The parent opposing relocation should further attempt to provide evidence that the new job could actually be located in the community where the parties currently reside. Consideration should also be given to the condition of the community in which the relocation is to take place. The home, other

---

Important Case: *In re Marriage of Burgess*
(13 Cal.4th 25) (Calif. 1996)

In this case, Wendy Burgess and Paul Burgess were divorced and living in the same community. The mother, who had temporary physical custody of their two children, wanted to move 40 miles away to take a new "career advancing" job and to provide better opportunities for the children. Although the father objected to this plan, the trial court awarded the mother permanent physical custody and allowed her to move to the new community.

The Court of Appeals disagreed, and said that in this type of case, the trial court should determine if the proposed move is "reasonably necessary" and determine "whether the benefit to the child in going with the moving parent outweighs the loss or diminution of contact with the nonmoving parent." The opinion of the Court of Appeals would have made it harder for custodial parents to move with their children to a distant location.

However, the Supreme Court of California reversed the decision of the Court of Appeals. The Supreme Court said the moving parent should not have to prove that the planned relocation is "necessary." If the custodial parent decides to move "for any sound good faith reason," the noncustodial, nonmoving parent would have to show it is "essential or expedient for the welfare of the child" to gain custody of the child. This ruling made it easier for custodial parents to move with their children to a new community.

---

surroundings, and schools should be considered. Proof in regard to friends who live in the new area, as well as any support groups would be vital. The parent who opposes relocation will hopefully be able to demonstrate how he or she has had continuous involvement in the raising of the child since the divorce proceedings, which can best be demonstrated by previous participation in school activities, religious activities, and various extracurricular events.

Courts across the country also look for the continuity of placement over many years, but in an increasingly mobile society, this factor has diminished in importance. There can also be proof presented by various mental health professionals, which can explain the psychological harm to the relocating child. The medical history of a child and the medical

---

Important Case: *Aaby vs. Strange*
(924 S.W.2d 623) (Tenn. 1996)

This case was a custody dispute between Gene Aaby and Judy Aaby Strange that arose when Judy, the primary custodial parent, wanted to move out of the State of Tennessee with their child to Kentucky. Gene and Judy were divorced in 1990. The court awarded custody of their son, Brandon, then 3 years old, to Judy, and the court awarded visitation to Gene. The judgment contained no prohibition against the custodial parent's moving out of the state with Brandon.

The dispute began when Gene filed a petition requesting his child support obligation be decreased. Judy filed a petition opposing the decrease and a request for permission to move with her son out of the state. Judy's reasons for the move was that she had remarried, she wanted to move closer to her new husband's family, and she had received a suitable offer for employment in Kentucky. Gene opposed the move stating a move would not be in the best interests of the child and sought to have custody of Brandon changed to him if Judy insisted on moving out of the state. Gene offered expert psychological and psychiatric proof that tended to show removal would not be in the best interests of Brandon. The experts based their conclusions in part on the relationships Brandon had formed with his father and the father's extended family. The trial court and the Court of Appeals agreed with Gene, but ultimately the Supreme Court of Tennessee agreed with Judy.

The Supreme Court ruled the custodial parent could remove the child in her custody from the jurisdiction unless the noncustodial parent showed, by a preponderance of the evidence, that the custodial parent's motive for moving was to defeat or deter the visitation rights of the noncustodial parent. That is, the court found that the mother's motive for moving was not vindictive. Also, the Court ruled that psychological and psychiatric evidence tending to show that the child could be harmed by the proposed move did not demonstrate a harm that was specific and serious enough to justify a change of custody.

---

care provided in the area of the proposed move should also be evaluated. If the relocating parent is truly interested in encouraging a positive relationship with the other party, then all efforts should be made to encourage frequent contacts and visits.

Legal Precedents

States have their own laws and legal precedents that might affect the decision by either the PRP or the NPRP to move away from the community where both parents previously lived. There has been a trend, however, for the courts to make it easier for the custodial or PRP to move to a distant location. In 1996, the Supreme Court of California took this position in a case called *In re Marriage of Burgess* (13 Cal.4th 25). In the same year, the Supreme Court of Tennessee made a similar ruling in the case called *Aaby vs. Strange* (924 S.W.2d 623). See page 107 for *Burgess* and page 108 for *Aaby*.

There may be more variation among the states regarding relocation than any other aspect of divorce and child custody and visitation. In many jurisdictions, the relocating parent has to prove both valid reason and no vindictive motive. However, expert testimony can be presented to prove that such a move is quite a difficult transition and can cause much stress to the child. The balancing of the PRP's needs versus the children's best interests in maintaining an ongoing relationship with the other parent also is considered in many states.

Principles To Keep in Mind

Maintain Time With Both Parents

When relocation occurs, the parents should devote their best efforts to developing a plan in which the amount of time the NPRP spends with the child is not significantly diminished. This can be accomplished by spending time with the child during school holidays as well as during an extended summer parenting time. Both parents need to work together to ensure this time with the NPRP is valuable. Also, hopefully the NPRP is committed to participating in events at the new location.

Importance of Consistency and Predictability

Children need continuity and consistency in order to feel secure in this world. They want and need both parents to be a constant in their lives, and it should be the goal of each parent to support these basic needs. What this means in practice is to cooperate in long-term planning, which involves looking ahead six to twelve months. Ideally, there should be identical calendars posted on the refrigerators of both parents' homes depicting the parenting schedule for the next several months. Most children can deal with the fact that time with the NPRP occurs

---

Relocation: Legal and Mental Health Perspectives

The National Interdisciplinary Colloquium on Custody Law is an independent group of practicing and academic lawyers, mental health professionals, and judges. They developed consensus opinions on a number of topics related to child custody and visitation and organized their conclusions in an important book, *Legal and Mental Health Perspectives on Child Custody Law: A Deskbook for Judges*, edited by Robert D. Levy (West Group, 1998).

When it came time to address how to handle the relocation of the custodial parent, these authors said, "Deciding these cases is painfully difficult: personal and deeply felt values, in the parents and in the judges, are implicated, because not enough is known about what is good for children, how to assess particular families, and the strengths and weaknesses of their parent-child relationships, as well as how to predict what impact any decision will have on each member of the family group and the family's interaction in the uncertain future."

The National Interdisciplinary Colloquium thought that state legislatures should develop laws based on principles such as the following:

• Generally, judges should not try to assess the motives of the relocating parent.

• There should be a presumption favoring the custodial parent's choice, especially when the relocation is to accept a significantly enhanced employment position or because of out-of-state remarriage.

• The relocating parent should guarantee, at his or her expense, the same visitation for the other parent as was previously allowed.

---

less frequently as long as they know what the schedule is. Once posted, it is important, of course, for the parents to stick to the schedule and not make last-minute changes.

What Goes Around Comes Around

Relocation of one of the parents puts a strain on the nerves of all the family members and also on the budgets of the parents. Moving can be quite expensive, and so is traveling back and forth several times a year. The cost of transportation for the child is an important issue that should be addressed by the parent who is proposing to relocate. Sometimes, the parents agree or the court decides the expense for the transportation will be borne by the parent who is moving. Sometimes, the parents share the cost and the time involved in the child's travel. For instance, if the father has moved to Chicago and the mother still lives in Lexington, Kentucky, they might agree to meet at the Burger King right off the Interstate in Indianapolis at 12 noon on Saturdays to hand off the child from one parent to the other.

When dealing with the practical and financial aspects of relocation, both parents should keep in mind, "Do unto others as you would have them do unto you." Before acting, put yourself in the other person's shoes. Ask yourself, "Would I appreciate such behavior?" and "What if I were at the receiving end of this decision?" When relocation occurs, working out the details of the parenting time arrangements seems to bring out the worst personality traits of both parents. It is usually a good time for restraint and patience, remembering the parents are going to have to deal with each other for another ten or twelve or more years—until the youngest child reaches age 18. It is a good time to think about how you would want to be treated if the situation were reversed. The Golden Rule rules!

Minimize Travel Headaches

In ideal circumstances, the child will look forward to visiting the household of the NPRP as an adventure, not a burden. There are many ways to achieve that goal, but usually the involved adults have to put some thought into how to bring it about. For extended automobile trips, waits in terminals, and air travel, there are games to be played. Since the whole point of parenting time is to spend time with the parent, we encourage interactive games (Uno and checkers for younger children; poker and chess for teenagers) rather than videogames. Rather than drudgery, a recurrent trip can be made into an enjoyable family ritual— by stopping at a special restaurant every time, keeping a journal, or organizing a scrapbook.

For some families, the way to make travel to a distant location an adventure is for the child to invite a friend to go on the trip. This suggestion is not intended for younger children, but it works well for adolescents. Since the visited parent might not be available 24 hours a day, it gives the teenager somebody to hang out with. For the teenager, it is more fun to explore new places if you're doing it with somebody. Some NPRPs do not like this idea because, "Parenting time should be for my child and me to spend quality time together, not for me to baby-sit somebody else's kid." However, such parents may not be aware of the great importance of peer relationships for adolescents. Some teenagers are uncomfortable and bored spending an entire weekend with a parent, but would enjoy spending a weekend with a friend and the parent together. Also, a parent can learn a great deal about his or her teenager by meeting the youngster's friends and seeing them interact together.

Stay In Touch

Compared to only a few years ago, it is much easier now for NPRPs to stay in touch with their children. Even young children know how to send and receive e-mails. Older children might enjoy creating a website with the help of the parent who lives in a distant city. The website might be "private," where only family members can post announcements, messages, and photographs, and only family members have access to it. Or, the website might be "public." That is, the child and the parent have some common interest—railroading, sailboats, recipes, soap operas, whatever—and they could create a website together that anybody with a similar interest might access. However, be careful not to share too much information about your child on an Internet website with public access.

Younger children usually have set times each week to talk on the telephone with the parent they are not currently living with. Many children and parents find these phone conversations to be awkward and unpleasant. The child will complain that her playtime is being interrupted, she doesn't have anything to talk about, she needs to be doing her homework, and so on. The NPRP will get frustrated and say the PRP is interfering with his phone calls and compromising his relationship with his child. If everybody works together and plans ahead, these phone calls can be enjoyable and constructive. For instance, the PRP can build the phone calls into the child's schedule and make sure the child is available at the time the phone calls occur. The child herself can make a little list of things to talk to Dad about, and keep it next to the telephone. The NPRP should do more than simply ask the child what happened at school that day. The NPRP should be aware of other aspects of the child's life—for example, hobbies, friends, scouts, music—and make conversation based on topics the child previously discussed. Also, these conversations should be give and take. The NPRP should be prepared to tell the child interesting information about his own life, not just ask the child questions.

Of course, among older children and teenagers cell phones are ubiquitous. The clever NPRP will find a way to use text messaging and voice mail to his or her advantage. Many children of divorce would probably enjoy an occasional "TM" or cell phone call from a parent, but these interactions should not be intrusive, controlling, or overly persistent. If the youngster feels the parent is calling too often, the offending person's phone number will simply be blocked from further access.

Even with the easy availability of e-mail, voice mail, and text messaging, one should not forget the power of old-fashioned snail mail. It is truly exciting for a child to receive a stamped envelope addressed to him or her. Short hand-written notes, cards, and photographs can be saved and savored in a way that is not possible for e-mail messages.

Negotiate a Win-Win Outcome

Herb's parents were divorced and Herb lived primarily with his mother. When Herb was 15, his father was offered a promotion at his company requiring him to move to another city. When the next parenting time occurred, the father frankly explained the situation to his son. He said, "Herb, I want to take this new job. It's very important to me. I'm sad that it means I'll be further away. But I want to work out something, so you'll get something for yourself out of my promotion. What do you want?" Herb said he wanted a motorcycle. He said it would be fun to visit his dad if he had a motorcycle. Herb's father cringed at the thought of his teenage son having a motorcycle, so they talked about various options. They eventually agreed on buying a small sailboat to be located near the father's new home. They both felt they benefited from the father's promotion, and they frequently used the sailboat together during the father's parenting time.

Mistakes to Avoid

The parenting behaviors in the following vignettes may seem ridiculous or implausible, but they really happened. Our hope is that divorced parents will learn from mistakes, both their own and the mistakes of others.

Failure To Give Notice

Josh's parents in Houston engaged in a bitter custody dispute that went on for years. When he was 8 years old, the court decided after a one-week trial that Josh would remain in his mother's custody. Josh's father was assigned visitation every other weekend, and the next scheduled visitation was to start a few days later on Friday at 6 p.m. However, on Friday evening Josh's father did not show up and he sent no message or any explanation for his absence. Josh's mother tried calling the father's home telephone number on Friday evening and over the weekend, but the phone was never answered. On Monday morning, Josh's mother called the father's office and learned—to her great surprise—that the father had taken a new job in Yokohama, Japan, and had already moved there! Josh, of course, was upset and confused. He did not know whether to be angry, sad, or both. Several months later, Josh received a letter from his father in which he tried to explain why he had left so suddenly without saying goodbye.

Being Too Rigid

In this book, we have generally advised divorced parents to be consistent, predictable, and fairly religious about sticking to agreements and schedules. That is good advice especially during the first year or so after a difficult divorce. During this time it is usually better to stick to the schedule and not make last-minute changes because there is a high risk that well-meaning flexibility will quickly turn into recurrent arguments over the parenting time arrangements. Although a moderate amount of rigidity may be a good thing during the early stages of a divorce, it is possible to have too much of a good thing. There are times when extreme rigidity and insistence on the previously established agreement turns into a bad thing. There are times when flexibility is to be admired, and inflexibility seriously undermines the child's relationship with one or perhaps both parents.

For example, every person in this country was affected to some degree by the tragic events of September 11, 2001. Children everywhere in the United States saw frightening images of airplanes crashing and people dying, and heard or overheard endless discussions of these happenings. At the time, Marjorie, age 11, lived with her mother near Memphis. Marjorie's father lived in San Diego and she visited him about once a month. The parents had agreed Marjorie would fly to San Diego for every three-day or four-day weekend, such as Labor Day, Columbus Day, and Thanksgiving. Since there were nonstop flights between these cities, Marjorie was able to fly as an unaccompanied child. Until September 2001, Marjorie very much enjoyed these trips to have parenting time with her father.

After 9/11, Marjorie became fearful of air travel. On the way to the airport for the Columbus Day weekend trip to California, she had a panic attack and the parenting time was canceled. Marjorie's father dealt with this situation in a remarkably intransient manner. He simply insisted that Marjorie come for the regularly scheduled parenting times, while Marjorie's mother refused to force the child onto an airplane. Moreover, the father refused to arrange for a family member to accompany Marjorie, refused to arrange alternative transportation, and refused to travel to Tennessee to have parenting time with his daughter close to her home. The next time they saw each other was when the father came to court in Memphis to pursue his wish to have parenting time on his own terms.

Too Long in the Back Seat

According to MapQuest, the driving time between Atlanta, Georgia, and Nashville, Tennessee, is about four hours. Jennifer, age 5, lived with her mother in Atlanta and had parenting time with her father every other weekend from Friday evening to Sunday evening and also every Wednesday evening. Because of the distance involved, the Wednesday evening parenting time never occurred. Jennifer's mother insisted that if the father wanted to see Jennifer for the weekend, he would need to pick her up in Atlanta on Friday evening and return her Sunday evening. On some occasions, the father picked Jennifer up and the two of them stayed in a local hotel for the weekend and had a good time. On other occasions, the father drove Jennifer back to Nashville for the weekend. Although the father tried to make the four-hour trips fun, they inevitably became tedious for Jennifer. She became very irritable during the travel time and then she started to resist going with her father in his car. Through her stubbornness, Jennifer's mother seriously compromised the girl's relationship with her father. Eventually, the court revised the schedule, such that the father had longer but less frequent parenting times.

Creating an Attractive Nuisance

Luke's favorite activity was to go fishing with his father. When his parents divorced, it was agreed Luke, age 8, would live with his father in Kansas City, Missouri, while his baby sister, Judy, would live with their mother in Topeka, Kansas. The driving time between these cities is only one hour. Since both children had parenting time with the NPRP every other weekend, it was intended that the children would spend every weekend together, either at their dad's house or their mom's house. However, there were times when Luke did not enjoy his parenting time at his mother's home—he had no friends in Topeka and he felt he had nothing in common with the baby, Judy. On weekends, wherever he happened to be, the baby got more attention than Luke.

As time passed, Luke became more and more resistant to visiting his mother in Topeka. Luke said, "All I want to do is stay home with Dad and go fishing." When Luke flatly refused to get in the car to drive to Topeka and threatened to run away from home, his father gave in and let Luke avoid spending the weekend with his mother. Since Luke seemed very unhappy, his father decided to cheer him up by taking him fishing. This incident turned into a pattern, and Luke rapidly learned that if he refused to have parenting time with his mother, he got to spend the weekend going fishing with his father instead. A family therapist worked with the parents to help them devise parenting time arrangements that would encourage both children to have satisfying relationships with both parents. Of course, the therapist quickly recommended the father not reward Luke by taking him fishing when he refused to have parenting time with his mother.

Moving Near and Far

When parents divorce, their children's lives are seriously disrupted. Divorce always involves somebody moving, and it may involve everybody in the family moving. When parents move away from each other and live in different communities or even different states, the children's lives continue to be disrupted on an ongoing basis. Although unnecessary relocations should be avoided, it is inevitable that many divorced parents will need to move for very good reasons. When this occurs, parents should put extra thought and effort into finding ways for their children to enjoy both parents, both households, and both communities.

Chapter Thirteen
Parental Rights and Responsibilities

Andy, age 14, was visiting his father for the weekend, who was the non-custodial parent. After they watched Saturday Night Live *together, Andy tripped on a rug, fell down, and cut his leg. The father took his son to the local emergency room late at night, where Andy's laceration was sutured. When Andy went home the next day, his mother learned of the injury and its treatment. It was basically a happy ending: the noncustodial father felt he had been a good parent; Andy felt he had a good dad; and the mother was relieved she had not been called to the emergency room the night before. This kind of event is a commonplace occurrence, but it has a serious flaw. According to the law in his state, the father as the noncustodial parent did not have the right to authorize the treatment; the hospital did not have the right to accept Andy as a patient; and the physician who put in the sutures could be charged with assault and battery.*

Since the relationship between divorced parents is often contentious, children suffer when they are victims of the ongoing dispute over both big and little issues. One issue that creates a great deal of misunderstanding and anger is defining the relative rights of custodial and noncustodial parents. The same problem occurs when we use the older terminology of custodial and noncustodial parents or when we use the newer terminology of primary residential parents (PRPs) and nonprimary residential parents (NPRPs). There is disagreement regarding this issue among professionals who work with divorced parents. There is a big difference between what is stated theoretically—for instance, the strict legal definition of the rights of noncustodial parents or NPRPs—and what happens in everyday practice.

We advocate the use of parenting plans and believe many of the angry misunderstandings between parents will be eliminated by this practice. The problem is there are many situations that may not be covered by the parenting plan, even one which has been thought out in a comprehensive manner. For instance, times change and the needs of a 17-year-old might not have been considered if the parenting plan was developed when he was 7. ("Guess what, Mom. Dad said he's getting me a motorcycle for Christmas!") Or, one parent tries to push into the territory apparently ceded to the other parent in the parenting plan. ("Of course, I agreed Jimmy's father would take him to religious education every Saturday and Catholic Mass every Sunday. But I can still take Jimmy to the Wednesday evening service at my Baptist church if I want to.") Or, circumstances arise when it is simply inconvenient to follow the letter of the parenting plan. In the example of Andy at the beginning of this chapter, Mr. Holmes did not have the right to authorize medical treatment, since it was not really an emergency, but he did it anyway.

There needs to be a framework for defining the relative rights of custodial and noncustodial parents. Although parenting plans should be individualized to the needs of each divorcing family, we believe there is room for consistent standards and guidelines. What we need in our society are basic, generally accepted ground rules for the most common post-divorce situation, when one parent is the custodial parent and the other is the noncustodial parent (or using the new terminology, the PRP and the NPRP). We believe it will be helpful to develop guidelines that divorcing parents, attorneys, judges, and therapists can apply in a consistent manner. If the rules of the game were more definite, each parent would have clearer expectations and would be less likely to feel cheated and resentful when he or she doesn't get what was hoped for. Ideally, the rules are made definite by placing provisions in the divorce decree, protecting both the custodial and the noncustodial parent.

Probably the most common source of disagreement between divorcing parents involves the details of the rights of the noncustodial parent or the NPRP. Some authorities say defining the rights of the NPRP is an unnecessary exercise. They say divorced parents are going to fight about something and if it turns out they cannot fight about the NPRP's rights, they will find some other battleground. We are not that pessimistic. However, we do think divorced parents need all the help they can get if they are going to cooperate in raising their children. One way to help these parents is to provide structure, to lay out clearly each parent's rights and responsibilities. Parenting plans provide this needed structure. We are suggesting that parenting plans follow general principles, as expressed in this chapter, so most divorcing couples will have approximately the same agreements regarding the parenting of their children. Readers should be aware of their local situation, since some state legislatures have developed a Bill of Rights for noncustodial parents.

Bringing some resolution to this issue would help therapists and medical personnel. If there were standardization regarding the rights of PRPs and NPRPs, it would help to structure and organize some aspects of divorce such as mediation, custody determinations, visitation evaluations, counseling for divorcing parents, and therapy for their children. We are saying it would be better if every divorcing couple did not have to reinvent the wheel when it comes to defining the NPRP's role in the child's life.

In this chapter "she" will be used to refer to the custodial parent or PRP and "he" to the noncustodial parent or NPRP. We are following that convention simply for clarity and for easy reading. There is no implication the mother is more suited or more likely to be the custodial parent or PRP.

Legal Opinions

Existing state laws and the higher courts have provided few guide-posts regarding the rights of the noncustodial parent (in states that still use such terminology). Some states no longer refer to "custodial" parents, but refer to residential parents or primary residential parents. The other parent is called the nonresidential or the nonprimary residential parent. States that have adopted the new terminology do not define the relative rights of the PRP and the NPRP. In fact, the relative rights are purposefully left vague, so the divorcing parents can define them for themselves. For the most part, this book has been using this newer terminology, such as the PRP and the NPRP. This particular chapter, because of the nature of the topic, will make use of both the older and the newer terminology.

In states using the traditional terminology ("custodial," "noncustodial," "visitation"), there is no comprehensive definition of the relative rights of custodial and noncustodial parents. A state law may simply indicate the custodial parent has responsibility for the child and it thereby suggests the noncustodial parent has no more rights regarding the child than a total stranger. These laws could lead one to believe the noncustodial parent may not take the child for medical treatment unless it is a true emergency and the custodial parent cannot be located. Of course, in a true emergency any person on the street could take the child to a hospital and seek treatment. Some states do define specifically the rights of the noncustodial parent. For instance, there may be a law providing the noncustodial parent the right to a copy of the child's medical records and the child's report card.

In 1986 a Court of Appeals in Virginia—in *Eichelberger vs. Eichelberger* (2 Va.App. 409)—addressed the question of how much latitude a noncustodial parent should have during visitation. The court said the noncustodial parent could provide whatever recreation he desired for the child, as long as it was not clearly dangerous: "Absent a finding by the court that the noncustodial parent has acted without concern for the child's well-being or best interest, has demonstrated irresponsible conduct, has interfered with basic decisions in areas which are the responsibility of the custodial parent, or finding that the activity which is questioned by the custodial parent presents a danger to the child's safety or well-being, neither the custodial parent nor the court may intervene to restrict activities during visitation." The court permitted the noncustodial parent to allow his child to ride a motorized dirt bike on the family farm in spite of the custodial parent's disapproval.

It is our impression attorneys (especially in states using the traditional terminology) give inconsistent advice regarding the rights of the noncustodial parent because it depends on who the client is. We think the attorneys' inconsistencies are a natural consequence of dealing in an adversarial setting with an issue that has no firm guidelines. It seems to us the attorney for the noncustodial father tells him he should take whatever prerogatives he can get away with, especially if the particular issue was not been spelled out explicitly in the divorce agreement. Conversely, the attorney for the custodial parent tells her she may have the right to limit the father's access to the child's school, pediatrician, therapist, and so on.

Physicians hear one thing from attorneys and something else from professional colleagues. Attorneys usually advise physicians to take whatever steps necessary to guard against the remote possibility of some future lawsuit. Many attorneys would recommend a doctor not treat a child without the permission of the custodial parent because there is some infinitesimal possibility he might be sued for assault and battery. This is not what happens in practice. It is more common for family practitioners and pediatricians to treat children at the request of noncustodial parents or NPRPs, stepparents, grandparents, and even babysitters.

General Principles

The way we address this problem is to start with a fundamental principle. It is usually in the child's best interests to feel that both of his parents love him, provide for him, and take responsibility for him. This means the noncustodial parent or the NPRP should be fully responsible when the child is in his charge.

The noncustodial parent or NPRP has greater rights than a babysitter, a full-time nanny, or the child's teacher. We need a systematic way to delineate the following gradation of authority over children:

• In states still using the concept of legal custody, the custodial parent has ultimate and absolute responsibility for and authority over the child.

• The noncustodial parent or NPRP has absolute responsibility for and authority over the child regarding most routine, day-to-day matters when the child is in his charge.

• Other individuals, such as babysitters and teachers, have more limited responsibility and more circumscribed authority over children in their charge.

• Total strangers have no responsibility or definite authority regarding other people's children, but they may choose to exercise limited authority in certain circumstances.

Recommended Guidelines

In this chapter we translate these basic principles into practical guidelines. The guidelines are not intended to be the last word in this discussion, but can be seen as an outline to be used by divorced parents, attorneys, judges, and therapists. These suggestions are not intended to advocate for any particular agenda, but hopefully reflect a balance between the interests of the child (to have a loving relationship with both parents), the right of the custodial parent (to have primary responsibility for the child), and the right of the noncustodial parent or NPRP (to have substantial shared responsibility for the child).

These guidelines are intended to take a common-sense approach to this question: How can two parents who greatly disagree with each other cooperate in raising a child? In developing these guidelines, we are assuming we are dealing with two responsible, capable, and nurturing parents. We are addressing the extremely common situation in which both parents are adequate, but one of them happens to have legal custody or primary responsibility for the child. The following guidelines or comments pertain to a number of routine situations ("I don't want my child visiting the home of his father's lying, cheating, no-good relatives!" and "The boy's mom signed him up for ballet lessons and is making a sissy out of him!"), as well as unusual situations ("I need to get Jimmy a tetanus shot so he can go to Boy Scout camp next week. His mom is on vacation in Latvia and we can't reach her to give permission.")

Extended Family

It is usually in the child's interests to maintain a good relationship with grandparents, other extended family members, and even the family friends of both parents. The implication here is one parent should not try to control the company the other parent may keep during his or her parenting time.

Many times this guideline is very hard to follow. If Mom has intense, legitimate animosity toward Dad, it is not unusual for her animosity to spread to Dad's parents, friends, and neighbors. Mom may hear innocent comments made by the father's family members and translate them in her mind to hateful, vindictive allegations. For instance, the child's paternal grandmother may say to the mother, "How's your new job coming?" The mother might take this to mean, "It's about time you found work. You've depended too long on the generous child support you receive every month."

We are not suggesting these feelings are always in the parent's imagination. No doubt there are some cases in which the other parent's relatives have truly been rude, inappropriate, or mean. We are simply saying the offended parent should not assume the child has been or will be offended by the other parent's relatives. It is almost always better for the custodial parent or PRP to let the child figure out for himself what he thinks and feels about the other parent's relatives. It may be necessary, of course, if the other parent's friends and relatives have truly been immoral or illegal, for the judge to limit the child's exposure to those individuals.

Education

In states with traditional child custody laws, the custodial parent has the right to make the major decisions regarding the child's education, such as where he attends school and whether to authorize special education placement. We suggest it is usually wise for the custodial parent to consult the noncustodial parent in these decisions.

In states making use of parenting plans, we suggest the plan specify that the parents will make every effort to discuss, collaborate, and agree on decisions regarding the child's education. If they come to an impasse, the parenting plan can say the custodial parent or PRP makes the final decision. If there is no parenting plan, these decisions may be addressed in the marital dissolution agreement.

It seems pretty obvious that it benefits the child to think both Mom and Dad are aware of his educational issues, have discussed his needs and plans, and generally have agreed. It certainly is good for the child to know both parents have visited the school, have met the teacher, have attended parent-teacher conferences, and have brought cookies for snack time. Of course, there are exceptions to almost every rule. Occasionally, there have been noncustodial or NPRPs who visited the child's school and became psychologically destructive. For instance, they may have told lies about the other parent or became extremely intrusive on the teacher's educational activities. If that were to happen, the custodial parent or, if necessary, the judge may need to limit the offending parent's contact with school personnel.

The topic of "Schools and Teachers" is discussed further in Chapter Sixteen.

Religion

Several courts have ruled that both parents—regardless of who has legal custody—have the right to take the child to church and enroll the child in religious education. One would think two reasonable parents would not subject a child to two totally different religious and philosophical points of view—but it happens and it is not unusual to see children who have been instructed with some combination of Protestant, Catholic, Jewish, and Mormon ideology. We do not see any easy solution to this problem. One might predict as adolescents these children will have great difficulty establishing a sense of identity and will become unusually cynical about religious issues.

Religion may become an issue if the parents are more concerned about what is easier for themselves instead of deciding what is best for the child. In many divorcing families, however, the parents are able to agree in the parenting plan that one of the parents will be primarily responsible for the religious upbringing of the children. Perhaps the parents agree that one of them will take responsibility for religious issues, while the other parent will take charge of educational issues. If the child had already been raised in a particular religion prior to the divorce, it probably is in the child's interests to maintain continuity with the same religion after the divorce. These suggestions seem simple and easy to follow, but there will always be parents who feel so strongly about religious issues they will consider themselves justified in violating whatever agreement they may have previously made.

Recreation

In the best of worlds, custodial and noncustodial parents will cooperate in promoting their children's extracurricular and recreational activities. For instance, the parents may alternate taking the child to soccer games. Another possibility is that the parent who is really invested in the child's piano lessons leaves work early two days a week in order to get the budding impresario to the music teacher. Meanwhile, the other parent thinks training in tae kwon do is very important, so he takes the child to classes every Saturday afternoon, including those Saturdays not scheduled for his visitation or parenting time.

On the other hand, parents may have widely different values and opinions as to how leisure time should be spent, so disputes will arise. It should be understood the noncustodial parent or NPRP has the right to provide his choice of recreation for the child, as long as it is not dangerous. Since our society offers a wide range of recreational activities and since people have such individual tastes, the custodial parent frequently feels like criticizing the noncustodial parent's choice. Usually, the solution to this problem is the custodial parent needs to give up some control and needs to accept life does present risks, the child may get scratched up if he goes body-surfing, or may get blisters if he goes on a long hike. When the child lives with the noncustodial parent or NPRP for an extended time over the summer, that parent should have the right on his own authority to enroll the child in a day camp or even an overnight camp.

Emergency Medical Care

One thing attorneys, doctors, parents, and judges agree on is noncustodial parents and NPRPs can take a child for emergency medical care. Of course, anybody at all can take a child for treatment of a true emergency. It is just common sense that this provision is in the best interests of the child.

Routine Medical Care

This is an area of confusion. Laws generally state the custodial parent or PRP is responsible for medical care; purists interpret these laws to mean the noncustodial parent has no authority at all in this area; but the common medical practice is to treat children at the request of noncustodial parents.

We think the noncustodial parent and NPRP should have complete responsibility for the child's routine needs when he physically has the child with him. This means the noncustodial parent and NPRP should be encouraged to provide basic medical care at home when the illness is minor and to take the child to the pediatrician when the illness is more serious. The noncustodial parent and NPRP should be able to authorize routine and reasonable tests, such as eye examinations, speech and hearing evaluations, x-rays, and laboratory tests. If the noncustodial parent or NPRP is sending the child to camp for the summer, the parent should be able to arrange for the precamp physical examination and to authorize medical care at the camp.

This approach is recommended because is it is good for the child to feel the noncustodial parent or NPRP is a complete parent, as much as possible. It is also more fulfilling for the noncustodial parent or NPRP to actually be in charge when the child is in his care, so he is more likely to put his heart into his time with the child. Finally, it really seems silly to require the physician in the situation regarding Andy, the boy at the beginning of this chapter, to telephone Andy's mother to get permission to suture the boy's laceration.

Serious Nonemergency Medical Care

The custodial parent alone should have the authority to make major medical decisions, including hospitalization, surgery, and invasive procedures, unless the parenting plan or marital dissolution agreement says differently. We suggest, for instance, a noncustodial parent might discover during the summer that his teenage daughter has scoliosis and could even take her to an orthopedic surgeon for a consultation and x-rays. Hopefully, the custodial and noncustodial parents would discuss together what to do next, but it would be up to the custodial parent to authorize surgery to correct the scoliosis. Of course, both parents should keep each other advised of the medical conditions of the children.

If the parents have agreed on a parenting plan, we recommend this issue be handled in the manner we discussed earlier in this chapter regarding educational decisions. Almost always the PRP and the NPRP would discuss and collaborate regarding serious nonemergency medical care. If they are not able to agree and an impasse occurs, the PRP would usually have the primary authority and responsibility regarding this issue.

Psychotherapy and Counseling

Psychiatric treatment, psychotherapy, and counseling are other kinds of "serious nonemergency medical care." Hopefully, the custodial and noncustodial parents (or the PRP and the NPRP) would agree on whether the child should be in counseling or should be taking some form of psychotropic medication, such as Ritalin or Adderall for attention-deficit/hyperactivity disorder. In fact, hopefully the therapist or psychiatrist would discuss these issues with both parents, not simply the parent who happens to bring the child for appointments.

If the parents are not able to agree, the use of psychotherapy or psychotropic medication would be handled the same as other forms of serious nonemergency medical care. That is, it would be up to the custodial parent or PRP to decide whether to initiate a trial of medication. Absent an emergency, it would usually be up to the custodial parent or PRP to authorize psychotherapy or counseling for the child. However, every attempt should be made to gather the thoughts of the NPRP in making these decisions.

Psychiatric and Psychological Evaluation

Most authorities say the noncustodial parent should not be allowed to take a child for any kind of psychological or psychiatric evaluation, unless it is an emergency. Accepting this point of view as a guideline does create a lack of symmetry, since the noncustodial parent could take the child for routine general medical care but not for routine psychiatric care. The reason for taking this position is the suspicion the noncustodial parent is consulting the psychiatrist or psychologist simply to collect evidence for a lawsuit to gain custody of the child. It is considered unethical for mental health professionals to see the child in those circumstances because it only encourages the noncustodial parent to shop around and arrange repeated evaluations until he finds a therapist who says what he wants to hear. One would hope both parents would agree to the treatment of the child's medical condition. The focus should be on the best interests of the child, not who is in control.

The De Facto Custodian

In some situations, the legal custodian has been out of the picture for a very long time and the child is actually being raised by the noncustodial parent. In such a situation the noncustodial parent should be allowed to make any and all decisions regarding the child. There is a way to avoid this awkward situation—which is to ask the court to make the person who is actually raising the child the custodial parent.

Common Sense

We live in a very bureaucratic society and children of divorce are greatly victimized by legalistic wrangling, arbitrary rules, unrealistic and unnatural schedules, and other people's agendas. Divorced parents, physicians, and therapists need to find ways to do what makes sense for the child and not dwell on the extremely remote prospect of being sued or criticized.

In the case of Andy, at the beginning of this chapter, we would say it was common sense for the emergency room physician to suture the laceration and not worry about calling the custodial parent to obtain permission for this routine nonemergency procedure.

Custodial and noncustodial parents need to share parenting responsibilities in a way that makes sense to the child. We mean the custodial parent should have the final word (if negotiation and agreement are impossible) regarding major educational, medical, and other decisions. The noncustodial parent and NPRP should be fully responsible when the child is actually with him, which may include making many routine educational, medical, and other decisions. The children of divorced parents will experience less confusion in their lives if our society develops a greater degree of standardization in the way custodial and noncustodial parents share their responsibilities.

Chapter Fourteen
New Relationships, Stepfamilies, and Blended Families

Magan, her mother, and stepfather moved from Los Angeles to Boston. The explanation for this major relocation given to the general public was that the stepfather was offered an attractive job opportunity in Boston. The real reason was that the family wanted to get away from Magan's biological father in L.A. The father was an offensive alcoholic who had been physically abusive to the mother and who continued to harass her long after their divorce. The father was a showy, flamboyant man who worked on the fringes of the motion picture industry.

In Boston Magan had two boyfriends. The first one was the bass guitarist of a rock band who had selected Magan to be his girl. The boyfriend dominated the relationship and took advantage of Magan both physically and psychologically. When they dated, Magan had to drive because the boy's license had been suspended for driving while intoxicated. Magan enjoyed being the girlfriend of a local rock star, but she disliked the boyfriend's drinking, his behavior, and his control over her. Magan gave the musician boyfriend an ultimatum to stop drinking, broke up with him, got back together again, and eventually broke up for good.

The second boyfriend in Boston was a classmate in her high school. He was polite, kind, good looking, and wealthy. He seemed too good to be true. The moral of this story is that children and adolescents are greatly influenced by the personalities and the events in their nuclear families and stepfamilies. Magan's relationships with her first boyfriend and the second boyfriend were echoes of the mother's relationships with the father and the stepfather. Perhaps Magan learned something from her mother's experience, that it is possible to have a satisfying, nonabusive relationship with a guy.

Divorcing parents frequently have very strong opinions about their prospects for moving on to a new, intimate, serious relationship. Sometimes "the other man" or "the other woman" is already waiting in the wings, so the new relationship is exactly the reason the old relationship failed. In this circumstance, one spouse is anticipating the end of the marriage and is eager to leave the old relationship and move on to a new relationship and perhaps a new family. On the other hand, the spouse who has been rejected may feel severely injured and have no interest in any kind of new, serious relationship for a long time.

In general, it is good to think in terms of moving on. Rather than considering oneself a perpetual victim, one should appreciate the process of healing and realize it involves moving on from being a victim to becoming a "survivor" and eventually a "thriver." Although there are many ways to survive and thrive, this usually means getting out, socializing, and thinking about remarriage as a real possibility. Since humans tend to be optimistic, divorcing individuals almost always fantasize the next marriage will be a whole lot better than the last one.

When a divorced parent starts thinking about a new, serious relationship, what should they consider for the children? Many people err by adopting one extreme position or the other. For example, some single parents involve their children in every aspect of dating: from planning encounters with prospective boyfriends or girlfriends; to being present during every dating activity; to assessing in detail the outcome of each date; and to collaborating in planning the next step in the parent's dating relationships. Some parents go to the other extreme—that is, the children do not get to meet the prospective stepmother or stepfather until the couple are actively considering marriage. We recommend a policy that is more middle-of-the-road. For example, we do not think the children need to be involved in or even aware of the first few dates a parent might have with a prospective boyfriend or girlfriend. However, if the dating relationship continues, it is wise to arrange many family-type outings that include the children so everybody gets to know each other.

Definitions

Stepfamilies or remarried families come about in three ways. Nowadays, the most common stepfamily history is that two parents divorced and then one or both of them remarried. Each time one of the parents remarries, a stepfamily is created. It does not matter whether the child is actually living with the remarried parent. If both parents have remarried, the child is part of two stepfamilies: one stepfamily includes his mother, his stepfather, and himself; the second stepfamily includes his father, his stepmother, and himself. The second way to create a stepfamily is when a parent has died and the surviving parent remarries. A third possibility is that an unmarried mother might later marry a man other than the child's father.

In any case, stepfamilies have certain characteristics: (1) All of the family members have experienced an important loss (of the former parent), whether through divorce or death. (2) There is a new person in the household (the stepparent), who may not necessarily fit in perfectly well. (3) From the child's point of view, there is a "missing" biological parent who is somewhere else. (4) The child belongs to two households with potentially conflicting messages and values.

A blended family is a type of stepfamily that is more complicated. For instance, two divorced parents may marry, both of whom already have children. You end up with both of the adults being a parent (to his or her own child) and a stepparent (to the spouse's child). Another way to create a blended family is for the parents of a stepfamily to have another child together. In this case, one child in the family still has a stepparent, while the other child has two biological parents in the same family. To add to the confusion, some people use inconsistent terminology and mix up stepfamilies with adoptive families and foster families.

Literary Allusions

Stepparents have not fared well in popular culture. The classic example was Cinderella's stepmother, who unfairly favored her own daughters over Cinderella. Of course, she ultimately got her retribution. Another example was portrayed in *The Stepfather,* a movie several years ago in which a man methodically and repeatedly married women who already had children. After an initial period of apparent stepfamily bliss, he would violently kill the woman and his stepchildren. He got his punishment also when one of the stepdaughters did him in.

Real life is not that dramatic. Many times, however, the child's relationship with the stepparent may affect and interfere with her relationship with her parent. For instance, there was a girl named Lorrie, whose parents divorced and both of them remarried. Lorrie had a very problematic relationship with her stepmother, who was rejecting and abusive. For example, she criticized the father when he bought Lorrie a small gift. The stepmother browbeat Lorrie to the point the two of them were not allowed to be home together without another person present. Although the girl previously had affection for her father, the continuing conflict with her stepmother eventually poisoned the relationship be-

---

Books for Stepparents

Dr. Emily Visher and Dr. John Visher collected a good deal of information about stepfamilies, based on their own personal experience, their clinical experiences as a psychologist and a psychiatrist, and their study of available research. They wrote an important book together that became a classic, *Stepfamilies: A Guide to Working With Stepparents and Stepchildren* (Brunner/Mazel, 1979). They also wrote *Stepfamilies: Myths and Realities* (Kensington Publishing, 1980) and *How To Win as a Stepfamily* (Taylor & Francis, 1991).

More recent books for the parents of stepfamilies and blended families include: *Stepcoupling: Creating and Sustaining a Strong Marriage in Today's Blended Family,* by Susan Wisdom and Jennifer Green (Crown Publishing Group, 2002); *7 Steps to Bonding With Your Stepchild,* by Suzen J. Ziegahn (St. Martin's Press, 2001); *Keys to Successful Stepfathering,* by Carl E. Pickhardt (Barron's Educational Series, 1997); *Blending Families,* by Elaine Fantle Shimberg (Penguin Group, 1999); and *Stepmotherhood: How To Survive Without Feeling Frustrated, Left Out, or Wicked,* by Cherie Burns (Three Rivers Press, 2001).

---

tween Lorrie and her father. On the other hand, Lorrie got along perfectly well with her mother and her new stepfather.

Free Advice for Stepparents

Stepparents receive a lot of advice, much of it unsolicited, on how to get along with the new stepchildren. The children's natural parent usually has some ideas about how they should deal with the stepparent. Sometimes grandparents, other relatives, and various friends get in the act. Not to be outdone, we wish to offer some suggestions to the parents of stepfamilies and blended families.

• Wait at least a year or two after your divorce before you remarry. Consider counseling regarding your stepchildren for yourself and your new spouse. Read some books about the problems of stepfamilies and blended families.

• Think about why you got married this time—presumably because you want a long-term relationship with a new spouse. If you truly love each other, you will find ways to accommodate each other's children. Understand your new role as a stepparent.

•   Feel good about just being yourself. Don't try to replace, make up for, or be better than some previous parent. Be careful not to take on too much responsibility, such as trying to be superstepparent and doing all the jobs belonging to the parents. Be sure you and your new spouse clearly define your new role as a stepparent.

•   Don't force yourself into a place in the child's heart when that spot is already occupied. For instance, don't insist the child call you Mom if the child already has a Mom. In fact, a good stepparent is usually comfortable with encouraging the child to relate to and respect the natural parent. This will help develop trust between you and your stepchildren.

•   Take your time to find out how you can best fit into the child's world. There will be important ways for you to shape the child's future, but you need to take some time to figure them out.

•   On the other hand, be prepared to assume a role that is very meaningful for the child. A 12-year-old boy who has known no father at all is going to have high hopes if a new stepfather arrives.

•   Put time and energy into building the foundation of a good relationship. Offer sincere compliments and show your appreciation to your stepchild. Arrange to do errands, activities, and fun events involving just you and the stepchild. The stepparent and the child might try to identify or develop a common interest that is special or different from their activities with other family members. Perhaps they both like science fiction or taking care of the dog.

•   Be respectful of the child's relationship to his parents, that is, to your new spouse as well as to his other natural parent. They may occasionally want their own time together. Try to spend individual time yourself with each of your children and stepchildren.

•   In a blended family the parents need to think through how they will parent together. They should sit down and talk about issues such as schools, financial priorities, and discipline. Talk over your ideas and philosophy regarding discipline prospectively, that is, before you actually need to.

•   Stepfamilies and blended families need to be unusually clear about communication. Don't take things for granted. Talk it out. Have family meetings—weekly, if possible. Try to sit down and have a family dinner at least two or three times a week.

•   In blended families, make sure the children are being treated fairly and equally. They are going to be sensitive to discrepancies. That does not mean the parents and grandparents need to calculate the value of presents down to the last nickel, to make sure each child gets exactly the same. This suggestion might mean, for instance, at Christmas the children get the same number of "big presents" and "little presents."

• When making introductions, don't refer to your spouse's children as stepchildren. They are all your children and don't want to be singled out.

• In your new family it is important to establish your own routines, rituals, and family traditions. See Chapter Eleven, "Holidays and Holy Days."

• Feel that you are a family, for better or for worse. When problems arise, look for solutions within the family. Don't jump to the conclusion that the solution is to extrude one of the children.

• Adolescents raise particular problems. Teenagers come and go, so they are not consistent members of blended families. They will have a developmental need to become physically and psychologically independent, which may be contrary to the blended family's need for cohesion.

Recycling

Being part of a blended family is a great opportunity to recycle and perhaps improve upon earlier relationships. If your first marriage was problematic, here's a chance to build a relationship on a firmer foundation. If you "blew it" when you raised your own children, perhaps you learned something and will fare better with your stepchildren. Orchestrating a stepfamily or a blended family can be a tremendously satisfying experience for the parent, the stepparent, and the children. If you do not believe us, just watch some reruns of *The Brady Bunch*.

Chapter Fifteen
Grandparents

*Marie was born in a small town in Oklahoma and lived there her entire
life. She had seven children and thirty-one grandchildren. Marie's home
was large and filled with love, laughter, and excitement when the family
gathered at Thanksgiving, Christmas, and the Fourth of July. Marie
cherished her place as a grandmother who provided affection with no
strings attached to her multitude of offspring.*

*Marie and her family attended church religiously—so to speak—and
participated in parish activities. Two of her sons and a grandson became
priests. Marie herself played the pipe organ at church almost every Sunday for more than fifty years, from the time she was a teenager until
shortly before her death. When she was at home and at her family's
parish church, Marie was respected and admired by every person she
encountered. But one day an odd thing happened when Marie attended
Mass in another community.*

*Marie had one of those charm bracelets in which the charms con-
sisted of little gold and silver tags. Each charm was engraved with the
name and birth date of one of Marie's grandchildren, so the whole device
became rather cumbersome as the number of her progeny increased. At
home, of course, the bracelet was a badge of great honor. However, the
odd thing happened when Marie left Oklahoma and visited relatives in
Massachusetts. Marie was attending Sunday Mass in a crowded church.
About half-way through the service, after the sermon, a person two rows
in front of Marie passed back a note which said, "Please don't jingle your
bracelet." The note surprised and shocked Marie, but it made her think—
that being a grandmother can be heroic in your own town, but in another
time or another place it can be offensive. Of course, that is the message of
this chapter.*

Grandparents are the spice of family relationships. Grandparents
can be a marvelous ingredient adding zest and tastiness to extended
families—and most of the time that is exactly what happens. But the

grandparent spice can ruin the whole meal if added at the wrong time or in the wrong amount.

Grandparents Can Be Positive

When parents divorce, grandparents can be enormously helpful. Grandparents can provide emotional support and sometimes financial assistance when a divorcing parent feels injured and abandoned by his or her former spouse. When parents divorce, they frequently find themselves back at their own parents' home for brief periods of time, or perhaps for longer periods. When this happens, it is usually a good approach for the grandparents to be supportive, sympathetic, and attentive listeners. Probably the best style is to be politely curious, but not overly nosey about the details of why the mom and dad split up.

When separation and divorce occur, grandparents can be particularly helpful to the children. This is especially true if the grandparents live nearby and have already been a regular part of the children's lives. Children of divorcing parents usually experience several months of unusual stress and tension. During this chaotic and confusing time, the grandparents can be a source of security and stability. There are many single-parent households in which grandparents help with child-care activities. The grandparents' home can be a peaceful and quiet place that seems distant from the disagreements and fighting that may occur in the child's family. In the best of circumstances, children and their grandparents give each other pleasure and comfort which is relatively free of conflict. Children make use of their grandparents as objects of identification, finding themselves adopting similar values and beliefs and sometimes similar vocations. Children make use of their grandparents as links to their family and community history.

In some families, the parents are unavailable and the grandparents take over the raising of the children. This may happen for many reasons: a parent is seriously ill or deceased; a parent has serious psychiatric or substance abuse problems; a parent is in prison; a parent's rights were terminated because of child abuse or neglect; or a parent has simply moved out of the child's life. Many times, grandparents take on this unexpected responsibility in a resolute and also joyful manner. This phenomenon appears to be increasing and it has been estimated that more than four million children live in households headed by grandparents and more than one million children are raised solely by grandparents. Custodial grandparents experience both physical and psychologi-

cal stress, especially if the grandchildren have serious medical or behavioral problems. Our society needs to find ways to support custodial
grandparents who are spending their retirement years attending teacher
conferences, supervising homework, and watching high school football
games.

Here are some situations in which grandparents played a particularly positive role in the context of parental divorce or serious family
dysfunction.

•   Susan, Alice, and Elizabeth were teenagers when their parents
divorced. Because of their father's career, the children grew up in several states and even lived three years in North Africa. As a result of
these frequent moves, the girls had no roots in any community and had
no long-lasting friendships. They were rolling stones gathering no moss.
However, the girls always maintained a relationship with their maternal grandparents. When the divorce occurred, the family went into emotional and financial decline—but the grandparents helped the girls
through this difficult time. They helped Susan apply to college and paid
her tuition. The grandparents also encouraged Alice to go to college and
paid her expenses. Although Elizabeth was just starting high school, she
went to live with the grandparents because her parents were too involved with their own problems to deal with her needs. In this family,
the maternal grandparents were happy to help the girls financially and
emotionally.

•   Betty and Butch had three children and all of them were divorced and remarried. This resulted in three blended families, which
included five biological grandchildren and seven "step-grandchildren."
Betty and Butch enjoyed good relationships with their three children
and their families and saw them often. It was remarkable that all
twelve grandchildren felt loved and appreciated in their grandparents'
home, regardless of whether they had an actual blood relationship
with Betty and Butch. The grandchildren noticed whose drawings
were on the grandparents' refrigerator and whose school pictures
were framed and hung in the family portrait gallery—they all were
included, of course. The children noticed and talked about the
birthday presents each of them received from the grandparents. Betty
and Butch were the kind of people who had enough love for each child
to receive a good share. As a final touch, Betty and Butch made wills
in which they named the twelve grandchildren and left a specific item
to each of them. Although Betty and Butch do not have much in the way

of worldly goods, each grandchild will receive something from them to treasure.

• By the time he was 4, Jimmy had already experienced enough tragedy for a life-time. His father was in prison for selling drugs. Then his mother died after an overdose of sleeping pills and alcohol, and it was never known whether her death was accidental or suicide. After his mother's death, Jimmy went to live with his maternal grandparents. The grandparents got in touch with Jimmy's father, who claimed he was rehabilitated in prison and that he planned to raise his son after his release. The grandparents started a regular schedule of taking Jimmy each month to visit his father in prison. The grandparents encouraged letters and phone calls. When Jimmy was 6, his father was released from prison. Jimmy continued to live with the maternal grandparents while his father proved himself by attending AA meetings, getting a job, and setting up a household. His father remarried. When he was 8, Jimmy was able to live with his father and stepmother, but he continued to enjoy the support of his maternal grandparents.

Grandparents Can Be Negative

Divorce is always a hard road and there are times when grandparents complicate everybody's life and make the situation worse than it needs to be. Here are some examples in which grandparents had a negative effect on divorcing families.

• On the one hand, grandparents might be overly critical of their child's parenting style or behavior in his or her marriage. For instance, Frieda wanted to divorce Harold because he patronized a sexually oriented massage parlor on two occasions. She took the legal steps to move out of the family home with her son (age 8) and daughter (age 6). Frieda and the two children lived for several months with the maternal grandparents. The grandparents incessantly criticized and badgered Frieda. The grandfather told Frieda—sometimes in front of the children—that Harold's extramarital activities were not so bad. After all, they were only flings with prostitutes and not full-fledged affairs. Also, the grandfather pointed out Harold had not contracted a sexually transmitted disease in the process. The grandmother criticized and second-guessed almost everything Frieda did with her children. When Frieda punished her son for being rude, the grandmother excused his behavior and advocated on his behalf. When Frieda took her daughter out to do some shopping, the grandmother said Frieda was spoiling the girl. Feeling overwhelmed and desperate, Frieda and the children moved out of the grandparents' home and checked into a motel.

• On the other hand, grandparents might be overly sympathetic to their child's point of view and take sides in a way that is destructive. When divorce occurs and the parents disagree over the plan for the children, one would expect grandparents to support in a general way the position of their own son or daughter. In this case, however, the grandmother involved herself in the dispute in a way that damaged her grandchild. That is, Julie, age 5, returned to her mother's home after weekend parenting time with her father and said, "Daddy hurt me when I took my bath." Julie's mother mentioned the girl's comment to the maternal grandmother, who immediately suspected child sexual abuse and decided to investigate. Julie's mother and grandmother turned on a tape recorder and started to question Julie about experiences at her father's house. They asked many questions about different forms of sexual touching, all of which Julie denied. One week later Julie spent another weekend with her father and afterwards the mother and grandmother turned on the tape recorder again and asked more questions about sexual touching between Julie and her father. Julie easily figured out what her grandmother wanted to hear, so Julie started describing sexual abuse by her father. The grandmother called child protective services, whose staff interviewed Julie and then insisted the father agree to a safety plan in which his parenting time was discontinued. It took child protective services several months to fully investigate the allegations and determine they were unfounded, since they had been caused by the grandmother's suggestive and repetitive questions. In this case, the grandmother's exaggerated loyalty to Julie's mother almost destroyed Julie's relationship with her father.

• Although it is unusual, sometimes the best parenting plan is for some of the children to live primarily with the mother and some to live primarily with the father. In such a case, Mr. Novell was the primary residential parent for his two sons, who were 9 and 11 years old. Ms. Novell was the primary residential parent for their baby daughter, age 2. Parenting time between the two households was arranged so that all three children were together about 80% of the time when the boys were not in school. (See Chapter Five, "Uncommon Parenting Arrangements.") The paternal grandparents lived nearby and had a strong relationship with Mr. Novell and their two grandsons. The grandparents faithfully attended the boys' performances at school and their soccer games. They took the boys to movies and invited them to spend the night at the grandparents' home. However, the grandparents ignored and essentially shunned their granddaughter. They seemed to associate the girl with Ms. Novell, whom they despised for divorcing their son. Although the little girl at age 2 did not realize what was happening, she surely felt like a second-class grandchild when she became a little older.

All of these six vignettes—both the positive and negative examples—illustrate how powerful grandparents can be. Grandparents are very important in intact families, but their effect is magnified when parents divorce or experience other major problems. Although grandparents are free to walk way from these tough situations, we believe most grandparents will want to intervene constructively when their children and grandchildren are facing a family crisis such as divorce.

Legal Precedents

In general, there are two situations in which grandparents become involved in legal disputes when parents divorce. First, grandparents can get involved in a child custody dispute with one or both of the parents. Second, the child could be in the custody of one of the parents and the grandparents might go to court to seek visitation or "grandparenting time" with the child.

Regarding custody disputes, in most divorces one of the parents is identified as the custodial or primary residential parent of the child. Occasionally, however, grandparents assert they are better qualified to have custody of the child. This circumstance may give rise to a conflict between two fundamental principles that come into play in such disputes. There is a basic principle that parents have a right to raise their own children, which means the parent would usually win a custody dispute over any "third party," including the grandparents. In fact, the Supreme Court established long ago that the Constitution protects the parents' right to establish a home and bring up children without interference by the government. There is a second basic principle the court should consider, "What is in the child's best interests?"

It is possible these two principles would be in conflict—for example, perhaps there is a custody dispute between a parent and grandparents (the third party) and it seems it is in the child's best interests to live

---

Important Case: *Painter vs. Bannister*
(140 N.W.2d 152) (Iowa 1966)

This case from Iowa was a custody dispute over Mark Painter, age 7. Two years previously, the boy's mother had died and the boy's father (Mr. Harold Painter) asked the maternal grandparents (Dwight and Margaret Bannister) to take temporary charge of the child. The father settled down, married, and wanted the child returned to his own custody. The local court awarded custody to the father. However, the grandparents appealed the case to the Supreme Court of Iowa.

The justices of the Iowa Supreme Court characterized the Bannisters' home as "stable, dependable, conventional, middle-class, middlewest...." They described the father's household as "unstable, unconventional, arty, Bohemian, and probably intellectually stimulating." Although the ultimate test was the best interests of the child, the Court also considered the right of the biological parent to have custody of his own child. The Court said that it considered a number of factors, including the trial testimony of a child psychologist.

The Iowa Supreme Court decided in 1966 the boy should stay in the custody of the maternal grandparents. They thought he was in a stable atmosphere and was happy and well adjusted. The justices also made a point of hoping the father would stay involved in the child's life. They said the boy "should be encouraged in every way possible to know his father. We are sure there are many ways in which Mr. Painter can enrich Mark's life."

---

primarily with the grandparents. A good example of such a case was *Painter vs. Bannister* (140 N.W.2d 152), in which the Supreme Court of Iowa decided the child should remain in the custody of the maternal grandparents rather than move to the custody of the father. Of course, the outcome of any new case would depend on local law, legal precedents, and the details of the particular child's and family's circumstances.

Regarding visitation disputes, grassroots organizations have actively advocated since the 1970s for new state laws to support grandparent visitation. All fifty states have enacted legislation related to grandparent visitation. Some state statutes are rather narrow in that they allow grandparents to petition for visitation only under specific circumstances. For example, if a parent died or a parent did not have custody of his or her children, the court may award visitation to the grandparents. On the other hand, many states allow grandparents to petition for visitation even if the parents are still married and living together as a family.

If a particular state does allow for grandparents to petition for visitation with their grandchildren, exactly what do the grandparents have to prove in court to win their case? At a minimum, the grandparent plaintiffs would need to prove the grandparents' visitation is in the child's best interests. Some state statutes are more restrictive—they require in addition proof that the child will be harmed if grandparent visitation does not occur.

For example, a case in Tennessee, *Hawk vs. Hawk* (855 S.W.2d 573), limited the rights of grandparents. There was a law in Tennessee allowing grandparents to have visitation simply by showing that such visitation was in the child's best interests. However, the Supreme Court of Tennessee said the law at that time violated the rights of the parents under the Constitution of the State of Tennessee to raise their children as they see fit. See the summary of this case on page 142.

Also, the state of Washington had an extremely broad statute that allowed not only grandparents but any person to seek visitation with a child in an intact family despite the wishes of the child's parents. This law was challenged and the case, *Troxel vs. Granville* (530 U.S. 57), eventually reached the U.S. Supreme Court. See the summary of this case on page 143. The effect of this case was to strengthen the rights of parents and somewhat weaken the rights of grandparents.

Suggestions for Grandparents

When parents divorce, it creates an opportunity for the grandparents to be a constructive influence on both the parents and children. Every situation is going to have its own special circumstances, but here are some suggestions for grandparents to consider.

• One of the basic messages of this book is that children of divorce should have a good relationship with both parents. Both sets of grandparents can help to achieve this goal. For instance, grandparents frequently have the occasion to make pleasant or positive comments about both Mommy and Daddy.

• Another basic message of this book is that children of divorce are damaged by high degrees of conflict and parents should avoid

Important Case: *Hawk vs. Hawk* (855 S.W.2d 573) (Tenn. 1993)

This case from Tennessee was a visitation dispute involving two children, and the dispute was between the children's parents and the paternal grandparents. Prior to the dispute, the children had a close relationship with their grandparents, who frequently babysat the children including overnight stays. However, a dispute arose between the parents and grandparents over issues such as discipline, the children's activities, and their bedtime schedules.

When the parents stopped the grandparents' involvement with their family, the grandparents sought court-ordered visitation under the Grandparent Visitation Act, which allowed a court to order "reasonable visitation" with grandparents if it was "in the best interests of the minor child." The trial court agreed with the grandparents, awarded them visitation, and added that the grandparents "don't have to answer to anybody when they have the children. . . . They can take the children anywhere they please, on vacation, and are not restricted as to where they can take them." The parents appealed the case to the Court of Appeals, which affirmed the lower court's decision. The case was then appealed to the Supreme Court of Tennessee.

In 1993, the Supreme Court of Tennessee agreed with the parents, that the lower court had deprived them of their rights under the Tennessee Constitution, which protects the privacy rights of parents in their child-rearing decisions. Parents have a fundamental right to raise their children as they see fit as long as they do not endanger the welfare of the children. The opinion stated that "an initial showing of harm to a child is necessary before the State may intervene to determine the 'best interest of the child.'" The trial court had inappropriately substituted its opinion as to the best interests of the children under the Grandparent Visitation Act, so the Supreme Court of Tennessee reversed the judgment that awarded visitation rights to the grandparents.

fighting over the children, in front of the children, and through the children. The same advice goes for grandparents. Grandparents may have very strong opinions about the children's mother, the father, the stepparents, the judge, the attorneys, and various other people involved with the family. Although they feel like sharing their opinions

---

Important Case: *Troxel vs. Granville* (530 U.S. 57) (2000)

This case from the state of Washington was a visitation dispute involving two girls who lived with their mother, Ms. Tommie Granville. Their father was deceased. The girls had a relationship with their paternal grandparents, Jenifer and Gary Troxel, and they continued to visit the Troxels after their father's death. However, a dispute arose between the girls' mother and the paternal grandparents. The grandparents wanted to have the visitation that their son would have had if he were alive, every other weekend and two weeks during the summer. Ms. Granville wanted to limit the grandparents' visitation to one day a month.

The Troxels took Ms. Granville to court, under the Washington law that provided, "Any person may petition the court for visitation rights at any time. . . ." Initially, the trial court agreed with the grandparents. However, Ms. Granville appealed the case to a higher court. The case made its way through courts in Washington and eventually to the U.S. Supreme Court.

In 2000, a majority of the Supreme Court agreed with the children's mother, Ms. Granville, and said the Washington statute made it too easy for the grandparents to override the wishes of the mother. In the Court's opinion, Justice Sandra Day O'Connor said, "So long as a parent adequately cares for his or her children (i.e., is fit), there will normally be no reason for the State to inject itself into the private realm of the family to further question the ability of that parent to make the best decisions concerning the rearing of that parent's children." Although the Supreme Court criticized the broad and expansive law in Washington as being unconstitutional, it did not say that all grandparent visitation laws are unconstitutional.

---

and their wisdom with their grandchildren, they should keep their mouths shut regarding highly charged topics such as the children's custody and visitation.

• Oftentimes grandparents can make their home into an emotional safe haven for their grandchildren. Since it is their home, they can make the rules, such as, "There will be no arguing between former spouses on these premises!"

• Although it is a tall order, grandparents can try to be neutral when the divorcing or divorced parents start fighting. The easiest way to express neutrality is to stay out of the fighting and let the parents work out their disagreements on their own.

•   Grandparents should seize the occasion to be "equal-opportunity grandparents." It should not matter if the child is a natural born grandchild, a stepchild, a foster child, or even a foreign exchange student living in the household. Share your love with each of them.

•   Grandparents may sustain a significant emotional loss if a family divorce results in greatly reduced contact with their grandchildren. Such an outcome can also be painful for the grandchildren. Try to avoid this future predicament by maintaining a civil relationship not only with your adult children, but also with their spouses.

•   If divorce or other circumstances result in the grandchildren moving out of town, find ways to stay in touch. Although e-mail is quick and easy, children love to send and receive real, old-fashioned mail in an envelope.

Chapter Sixteen
Schools and Teachers

Billie Jean, age 3, was enrolled in the Happy Hours Preschool when her parents separated and started the process of divorcing. A custody dispute ensued and the temporary arrangement was for Billie Jean to live alternating weeks with her mother and her father. Both of the parents liked the Happy Hours Preschool and it was good that Billie Jean could continue there, since at least part of her day had a sense of stability to it. Billie Jean's teacher, Ms. Edmondson, tried to stay in touch with both parents.

Ms. Edmondson noticed Billie Jean was quite different each week and it seemed to be related to which parent she was living with at the time. When she was living with her mother, Billie Jean was more likely to seem irritable, manipulative, and overly demanding. When she was living with her father, Billie Jean was more pleasant and simply blended in better with the other children. What struck Ms. Edmondson the most was how differently her parents behaved and how Billie Jean related to her mother and father, when each parent dropped her off in the morning.

Billie Jean's mother followed an unpredictable schedule and dropped the girl off at a different time each day. The mother frequently seemed harried and disorganized. On one occasion the mother was wearing nightclothes and a bathrobe when she delivered Billie Jean to nursery school. It was most striking how the mother made a very big production out of the simple process of dropping off her daughter. She hugged Billie Jean many times, gave her many reassurances, and usually had many instructions for Ms. Edmondson. The result was Billie Jean always became emotionally upset at the separations from her mother, so the mother had to hug her a few more times. Ms. Edmondson also noticed at the end of the day when the mother came to pick up Billie Jean, the girl was almost indifferent and seemed more interested in continuing some play activity rather than going home.

Ms. Edmondson observed a different pattern when Billie Jean's father dropped the girl off. The father came at the same time every day, gave Billie Jean a hug, said goodbye, and left. Billie Jean was not upset, but readily got involved with the activities at the preschool. At the end of the day Billie Jean ran to greet her father and was eager to go home with him. Ms. Edmondson had several conversations with the father, and thought he was very interested in comparing notes regarding play activities for young children, discipline, and other aspects of parenting.

When the custody dispute eventually came to court, both the mother and the father wanted Ms. Edmondson and other personnel from Happy Hours Preschool to testify. Ms. Edmondson preferred to keep out of the parental conflict, since she wanted to stay on good terms with both parents. She ultimately did testify, but did it in a way that was comfortable for her. The teacher simply testified about the things she had observed, the repetitive behavior patterns of the mother, the father, and of Billie Jean. Ms. Edmondson did not draw any conclusions about who the better parent might be and did not have any suggestions or recommendations to make. She merely described what she had seen. The judge took Ms. Edmondson's observations into consideration, along with much additional information, and ruled the father should have custody of Billie Jean.

Since school is such an important part of the lives of all children, it is easy to see how teachers and school administrators are likely be very aware of the experiences of children of divorced parents. Teachers are in a wonderful position to be helpful to these children, although it may seem to go beyond their basic job description. Teachers, guidance counselors, and principals relate to children of divorce in many ways: as part of the support network for children of divorce; communicating with two sets of parents in different households and perhaps different communities; coping with two parents, who might be quite hostile to each other; and perhaps dealing with subpoenas and other legal issues.

School as Support Network

School is an important part of the support system for children of divorce because sometimes school is the only calm, predictable, sensible, and pleasant place for the child to be. Teachers can be helpful in many ways. For example, if a child seems unusually upset, the teacher might try to be reassuring and check with the youngster privately to see if he wants to talk about something. At some point it might be helpful to let the child know it is fine to talk in classroom discussions about di-

vorce, arguments, stepparents, and similar subjects. This does not mean
the teacher is trying to do psychotherapy. It only means the teacher is
communicating it is fine to talk about subjects that seem touchy and
sensitive—because many other children have had the same experiences
and it is useful for the child to discover that.

Teachers can also be helpful by letting children know, during the
normal course of classroom activities, there are many kinds of families.
Some children have two parents; some have one parent; some have a
stepparent; some are raised by grandparents. The point is all of these
families are fine and children do not need to assume the only right way
to grow up is to have two parents in the same household. We are not
suggesting the teacher should give a lecture on this subject. On the
contrary, there are many opportunities during everyday classroom activities to express this message.

For example, young children frequently draw pictures of their family members, either spontaneously or at the suggestion of the teacher.
The pictures may provide a wonderful opportunity for the teacher to
compliment the children's artistic abilities, but also to help them express the relationships of the people in their family and to understand
there are many acceptable ways to organize people in a household. Another opportunity may arise when the children hear a story in school
about a divorced family. While respecting their right to privacy, the
teacher might ask if there are any children in the classroom who live
with a stepparent or a foster parent. The children might find it helpful
to compare their own experiences with the characters in the story. Many
times children describe their emotional upheavals in their writings. Great
insights can be gained from reviewing these efforts.

In order for the teacher to be helpful, she needs to know what is
happening in the child's life. For younger children we think it is a good
idea for parents to let the teacher know if something unusual has happened in the family. This includes items such as parental separation or
divorce, the death of a grandparent, and the serious illness of a sibling.
This knowledge allows the teacher to be sensitive and to understand
why a child is behaving in a particular way. With that understanding,
the teacher does a better job at teaching and developing appropriate
behavior patterns in children.

In many elementary schools the guidance counselors are very much
aware of the family arrangements of the children under their purview.
Some school counselors have found it helpful to have group meetings
for children of divorce. There are a number of wonderful materials avail-

able to assist the professional when facing these issues. The counselor should check first with the parent, of course, before including a child in such a group.

Counseling groups are probably helpful because the child learns other youngsters have had similar experiences. We think some of these group counseling meetings would consist of open-ended discussions; some would involve the children relating events that happened at home; in some meetings the children might draw pictures of family members engaged in happy or not-so-happy activities; and in some meetings the counselor would give direct advice. For example, the counselor might encourage the children to try to stay out of conflict between the parents. If it seems possible to achieve, the counselor might encourage the children to try to have a satisfying and affectionate relationship with both parents.

Communicating With Parents

In Chapter Thirteen we emphasized how both the PRP and NPRP —or the custodial and noncustodial parents—should be actively involved in the day-to-day work of child rearing, not just in arranging for quality time. How should this general principle apply to the child's education? We think both parents should be aware of educational issues, should meet the teachers, should be fully informed about the child's progress, and should go to PTA meetings. A positive relationship between both parents and the school system helps the child tremendously.

If for some reason the parents do not agree, the custodial parent or PRP will be primarily in charge unless the divorce agreement or parenting plan states otherwise. If the parents can not agree, the custodial parent or PRP will likely make the decision that the child will attend School A rather than School B, will decide whether the child takes a sandwich or buys lunch in the cafeteria, and will authorize for the youngster to be in special education, if that happens to become necessary.

Since both parents should be involved as much as possible in educational issues, school administrators must exert extra effort these days to know about and communicate with both the mother and father. When the child is registered at the beginning of each school year, the school office should collect accurate information regarding the following:

With whom does the child live?
Who has primary custody or who is the PRP?
Names, address, and telephone numbers of mother and stepfather.

Names, address, and telephone numbers of father and stepmother.
Who should receive report cards?
Who should receive other notices and school newsletters?
Who will be the primary contact person with the teachers?
Who is authorized to pick the child up from school?
Who should be called if the child is sick?

The experienced school administrator can probably think of a few more questions that are good to ask. Basically, it is useful to clarify the ground rules at the beginning of the year rather than several months later when the paternal grandmother suddenly shows up in the middle of the day to pick up the child.

It is our opinion the child's school should send identical correspondence to the PRP and the NPRP, which includes report cards, announcements of meetings, and school newsletters. The PRP parent should ordinarily take care of the day-to-day communication with the child's teacher, but the NPRP parent should at the very minimum have the opportunity once or twice during the school year to meet with the teacher.

We are sure the suggestions in this chapter are not practiced everywhere. Educational policies and procedures are determined, at least in part, by state law, so the usual practice may be quite different from state to state. For example, in Tennessee there is a state law requiring that NPRPs have access to the educational records of their children. As a result, most schools in Tennessee automatically send report cards and other information to both parents. On the other hand, the practice in Oklahoma is almost the opposite. That is, schools do not send anything to the noncustodial parent unless the divorce decree requires school information be sent to both parents. Parents should not rely just on state law but try to be actively involved in school activities. Sit down with the appropriate school administrator and work to develop appropriate rules. Hopefully, both parents and stepparents can work together on this issue.

Playing Referee

Just as a child may be caught in the middle between two battling parents, the child's teacher may be in the same spot. The divorced parents may both try to win the alliance and the loyalty of the teacher. Both parents may be very demanding and try to talk the teacher into accepting their respective arguments. They may insist on completely contradictory agendas for the child. They may resent the fact the teacher has had communication with the other parent. What should the beleaguered teacher do?

• First, the teacher should be sure to get the school administrator and school guidance counselor involved early on in the process.

• Often, the teacher should follow the same advice given to the child, which is to stay out of the fighting. When the mother starts to complain about what an imbecile the father has been, the teacher can directly say she is not interested in getting involved in discussing that topic.

• If there is any confusion about the issue, the teacher should be clear about which parent to contact regarding everyday situations. If Jimmy has not done his homework, she should ordinarily touch base with the custodial parent or PRP, who has responsibility for sorting out routine educational issues. It is too much to expect the teacher to notify both parents about every little thing in the classroom.

• It does make sense, however, to have a system of notifying both parents about many events at school: the periodic parent-teacher conferences; the class play; the holiday musical. The implication is the teacher will have to develop a more elaborate communication system than simply sending a note home with Jimmy. She will need to have a mailing list for the parents of all her students. Some of those letters can go home with the students. Other letters will be mailed, such as the copies to the NPRPs. Hopefully this additional cost can be absorbed by the school instead of the individual teacher. With today's technology, e-mail can be an important tool in communicating with both parents.

• The teacher should figure out the best method for her regarding the parent-teacher conferences. It is our impression most of the time, when parents are divorced, it is best to try to meet with both of the parents at the same time. This obviously saves the teacher some time and it makes it possible to make the same statement to both parents at the same time, which reduces possible misinterpretations and miscommunications. Stepparent participation is also useful if the teacher is convinced a positive parenting atmosphere exists among the parents and stepparents.

• On the other hand, sometimes divorced parents are so angry at each other it is pointless to have them in the same room at the same time. There is so much hostility the teacher will not be able to accomplish anything with either parent. In such a case, it becomes necessary for the teacher to schedule separate parent-teacher meetings. This is not fair to the educator but many times it is a sad reality.

•   What about important meetings that only happen once? An example would be the meeting with special education personnel to discuss an individual educational plan. It is important for the person organizing the meeting to make sure the parent will be there who has the authority to make decisions regarding educational issues. It is usually helpful for the second parent to be present also, as long as the meeting does not turn into an argument between the two parents. These parents need to be a united front when dealing with a child's educational problems.

•   What about attendance at school events, such as the class play? Should both parents attend these occasions? This can be a problem if the child senses friction between the parents. The issue is the child may feel uncomfortable being affectionate and pleasant to both parents at the same time, especially in a public setting. In the worst scenario, the child may totally ignore the "other parent" or be very rude. The situation becomes uncomfortable for everybody. If this is the current situation, it might be best for the parents to agree to take turns attending these school events.

Teachers and school counselors have the opportunity to provide stability and self-respect to children of divorce, which they may sorely need. The children may find their time at school is an island of tranquility compared to their home ports, which are very troubled. Although it is not the responsibility of school personnel to compensate for every child's serious family problems, teachers can be very helpful by being aware of the issues facing children of divorce and making small accommodations.

Chapter Seventeen
Mental Health Professionals

Ms. Sears had custody of her 14-year-old daughter, Sally, who had anorexia nervosa. There appeared to be a symbiotic relationship between mother and daughter and both of them felt it was important for Sally to be as perfect a child as possible. The girl was in therapy with a child psychiatrist, who was also seeing the girl, the mother, and stepfather in family therapy.

The father, Mr. Roebuck, sought custody of Sally and the case went to court. The child psychiatrist agreed to testify and recommended custody remain with Ms. Sears and the stepfather. The court upheld this recommendation. Since the child's therapist had said in court the mother should be the custodial parent, Ms. Sears took the psychiatrist's testimony as unequivocal endorsement of her values and her parenting skills. Since she was doing such a good job, she decided to discontinue Sally's therapy. After all, a highly credentialed child psychiatrist had stated under oath that Ms. Sears was a good mother. The anorexic girl later required both medical and psychiatric hospitalizations, but the mother steadfastly maintained her family had received the official stamp of approval.

In other words, the child's emotional condition worsened and her therapy was damaged because her therapist had agreed to testify regarding the custody dispute. She probably would have been better off if the therapist had stayed out of the dispute altogether.

Sally, Ms. Sears, and Mr. Roebuck will reappear later in this chapter.

Since about one-half of marriages in the United States end in divorce, there are many children and adolescents whose parents are separated, divorced, and perhaps remarried. Many of these children and their families have had the occasion to see mental health professionals for one reason or another. The purpose of this chapter is to explain the various roles a mental health professional might play with the children of divorce. It is important to understand these roles are quite distinct from each other. When a divorced parent starts seeing a mental health

professional, it is important for both of them to clarify exactly what
assistance the parent is seeking.

Defining the Mental Health Professional's Role

There are several ways in which a mental health professional might
be involved with children of divorce and their family members.

As a Therapist for the Child
The therapist may be seeing a youngster, whose parents are cur-
rently divorcing, or could be treating an adolescent, whose parents di-
vorced many years earlier but whose emotional wounds are still tender.
In the example at the beginning of the chapter, the psychiatrist was
Sally Roebuck's therapist.

As a Therapist for One of the Parents
Because the process of divorce creates such an emotional upheaval,
many divorced parents find it helpful to have individual or group counseling.

As a Family Therapist
The mental health professional may become the therapist for the
new family created following the divorce. He may become the therapist
for a blended family or some other complex combination of parents,
stepparents, half-siblings, and stepsiblings. In the example, the psychiatrist was also the therapist for the Sears family.

As an Expert Witness
The mental health professional may be asked to do a custody evaluation. In some custody disputes, one or both sides or the court itself
arranges for the parents and the children to undergo a custody evaluation by a mental health professional, usually a psychologist or a psychiatrist. The purpose of this evaluation is to determine what custody arrangement is in the best interests of the children and to make recommendations to the court. In the example, the psychiatrist also became
an expert witness, in addition to being a therapist.

As a Divorce Mediator
A professional divorce mediator has studied both the psychological
and the legal ramifications of divorce. It is his job to help the parties

negotiate and agree on property settlement, custody, and visitation arrangements. Divorce mediation is discussed more in chapter eighteen.

As a Counselor for the Divorced Parents

The divorce counselor is a mental health professional who tries to help the parents find ways to raise their children in a cooperative manner. The basic mission of divorce counseling is to help parents avoid grinding the children up in the course of their own disputes. Divorce and visitation counseling is also discussed in chapter eighteen.

As a Scholar and Researcher

Some mental health professionals do not directly evaluate or treat individuals or specific families, but study large numbers of families through systematic research. This is especially true of psychologists, whose research helps us understanding what happens to individual children by studying the big picture, i.e., monitoring many families over many years. See the box on page 155.

In the case of Sally Roebuck at the beginning of this chapter, the psychiatrist became involved in three different roles: as the therapist for Sally, the therapist for her family, and also as an expert witness at her custody trial. That was a mistake. The anecdote illustrates how important it is for the therapist to be extremely careful in keeping his role precisely defined. It is important for the therapist to not attempt to wear too many hats at once.

There are many roles mental health professionals may take, so a therapist's job may change as the divorce process moves forward and the family's needs change. The transition from one role to another does not always work. In fact, in some situations, the therapist should make it absolutely clear he cannot assume two different roles at the same time. It is very hard, for instance, for a psychiatrist who has already been functioning as the child's therapist to change hats and become an unbiased professional to perform a custody evaluation and to make recommendations to the court regarding custody and visitation. It would seem very hard, also, for one psychologist to be the individual therapist for two parents who are getting divorced from each other.

In other situations, a professional may be able to work with a client or a divorced family in more than one way. For instance, a psychologist might become involved with a divorcing family by doing a custody evalu-

Research Regarding Children of Divorce

There has been an enormous amount of research by psychologists and sociologists regarding divorce and its effects on the children. Probably the two best known scholars of this topic are Judith Wallerstein (from California) and E. Mavis Hetherington (from Virginia). In general, Dr. Wallerstein emphasized in her writings the unhappy consequences of divorce on children both for the near term and many years later. On the other hand, Dr. Hetherington put a more optimistic spin on her findings, in that she concluded that 75% of children do well after living through divorce.

Judith Wallerstein, Ph.D., and Joan B. Kelly, Ph.D., designed a major longitudinal study of the responses of normal, psychologically healthy children and their parents to divorce. Their research involved 60 families and was known as the California Children of Divorce Study. The children and their parents were interviewed at the time of marital separation and periodically for the next 25 years. The original study was described by Wallerstein and Kelly in *Surviving the Break-up: How Children and Parents Cope With Divorce* (Basic Books, 1980). The 10-year follow-up was described by Wallerstein and Sandra Blakeslee in *Second Chances: Men, Women, and Children a Decade After Divorce* (Ticknor and Fields, 1989). The 25-year follow-up was published in *The Unexpected Legacy of Divorce: The 25 Year Landmark Study* (Hyperion, 2001), by Wallerstein, Sandra Blakeslee, and Julia Lewis.

E. Mavis Hetherington, Ph.D., devoted her career to studying how children cope with their parents' divorce. She and her colleagues at the University of Virginia designed several large studies involving hundreds of families and followed them for as long as 20 years. She compared the divorced families with intact families. Overall, she found that about 25% of children of divorced families experienced major problems or emotional difficulties, compared to about 10% of children in intact families. Hetherington and co-author John Kelly published an overview of her research in *For Better or for Worse: Divorce Reconsidered* (W. W. Norton, 2002).

ation and during the evaluation she has had the opportunity to meet and get to know both parents. Or she may have been a mediator who helped the parents negotiate an agreement regarding the property and the children. If both parents have come to respect and trust the same psychologist, the situation could evolve to where the psychologist becomes the divorce counselor and continues to help the divorced couple work out the details on an ongoing basis. It is also conceivable after the evaluation was over and the legal issues had been fully resolved, the psychologist who did the custody evaluation might become the therapist for one of the children. This would make particularly good sense if *both* parents still respected the psychologist's work.

Defining the Therapist's Mission

Any mental health professional who evaluates, treats, or counsels any member of a divorcing or divorced family should have a crystal clear understanding of his role. After his role is defined, he also needs to clarify what his mission may be within the role. After agreeing on what the assignment is, somebody should say to the mental health professional, "That is your mission, if you choose to accept it." Basically, the therapist will do a better job if he knows what his client is expecting of him. This process of clarifying both the role and the mission is the joint responsibility of the mental health professional and the client. As a good consumer, the prospective client should be aware of exactly what he or she is asking the therapist to accomplish.

What exactly are the missions a therapist may be asked to accomplish? In treating a child of divorced parents, for instance, the therapist may be expected to help the child be more happy, less worried, better behaved, and more successful in school. In most divorced families it should be understood the purpose of the therapy is to help the child love and respect both his parents. Usually it is up to the therapist to clarify this point, that the purpose of the counseling is to help the child have a happy, comfortable, and satisfying relationship with both parents. It may be important for the therapist and both parents to discuss this subject explicitly at the beginning.

In some divorced families, the purpose of the child's therapy may not be to help the child have a satisfying relationship with both parents. In fact, the purpose of the therapy may be just the opposite. For instance, it may be the child's NPRP has withdrawn from the relationship, has no interest in keeping in touch, and it is unlikely he or she will ever change. Sometimes children have extremely elaborate wishful fantasies about the whereabouts, careers, and intentions of the parents who have abandoned them. In such a situation, the therapist may need to help the child accept that the NPRP is not going to match up to the child's fantasies.

Signals of Emotional Distress

Children react to the stress of parental divorce in many ways. If the youngster is having serious symptoms, he many need evaluation by a mental health professional. In some cases the counselor may be able to help the child through a crisis by having only two or three meetings. In conducting the evaluation, the counselor may ask the parent about symptoms like these:

Worrying Too Much

A child's emotional distress may be manifested by continuing anxiety, fearfulness, and related symptoms such as repetitive nightmares.

Not Worrying Enough

Some children distance themselves from family events and family conflict and act as though they are not involved or bothered by these issues. To some extent, this kind of defense mechanism may be adaptive and useful for the child. However, if the child totally denies any interest or concern about serious family events, it may mean he is not dealing with his feelings in a healthy way.

Depression

This is the most common response to divorce and other serious family problems. The child may be apathetic, tearful, and obviously unhappy. His depression may be more subtle. For instance, it may be manifested by withdrawal from family social events and a lack of interest in activities ordinarily considered fun.

Physical Symptoms

Sometimes stomachaches, headaches, and more dramatic symptoms such as fainting spells may be signs of emotional problems in a child or adolescent.

Oppositional and Disruptive Behaviors

When a child who is usually pleasant and compliant is put under stress, especially stress related to family conflict, the youngster may become argumentative and oppositional. Sometimes children manifest

their emotional distress by delinquent behavior such as fighting, steal-
ing, and breaking rules.

Deterioration in Usual Level of Functioning

This deterioration may mean the loss of a developmental skill already achieved, such as fecal soiling by a young child who had already
been toilet trained. It could mean very poor school grades by a youngster who previously had been a good student.

Implications for Psychotherapy

When helping the child or adolescent deal with parental divorce the
therapist may find it helpful to be more directive than usual. For instance, the youngster may find himself being sucked into the parental
conflict. He may find himself actively allying himself with one parent
and rejecting the other. He may feel it is his job to negotiate both big
and little issues between the parents. Since the divorce makes his parents miserable, he may think it is up to him to make them happy. It is
usually good to advise the child to stay out of the fighting and to try to be
reasonably neutral. This may be hard to accomplish since the parents
may be campaigning for the youngster's vote and affection.

Therapists may see youngsters whose parents divorced many years
earlier and are now referred for a completely separate reason. In such a
case an adolescent may appear open and nondefensive about the details
and the circumstances of his parents' divorce. He is likely to say some
form of: "It really doesn't bother me. . . . It was a long time ago. . . . It
doesn't matter anyway, since there's nothing I can do about it." The
therapist who pursues this matter patiently will probably find the divorce really does matter in many ways. The youngster is likely to feel
resentment because most of his childhood and adolescence has been
compromised by his parents' needs and preferences. He has repeatedly
had to accommodate his schedule to theirs, to move from one household
and community to another, to maintain a fragile relationship with the
noncustodial parent through visitation, to adapt to stepparents, and to
give up the closeness and simplicity of an intact nuclear family.

You Need Two Heads To Wear Two Hats

The most common dilemma for therapists in the context of a custody dispute is to be asked to take on two conflicting roles at the same

time. For example, suppose the psychiatrist, social worker, or psychologist has been asked to perform an independent custody evaluation. Such an evaluation usually consists of assessing the youngster and both parents and making recommendations intended to be in the best interests of the child. Suppose the mental health professional has already been involved as the therapist of the child or of one of the parents. In these situations a professional may choose *either* to be the evaluator *or* to be the therapist, but it rarely works to try to do both at the same time. When a new client is referred for evaluation, it is helpful to clarify from the outset whether one's role is to conduct an evaluation for the use of the court or to conduct a clinical evaluation and provide therapy.

It is not unusual to already be treating a child or an adolescent at the point when the parents embark on a full-fledged custody dispute. It almost always happens that the PRP, who was the parent who brought the youngster for therapy in the first place, and the PRP's attorney ask the therapist to become actively involved in the custody dispute. Usually this means for the therapist to write a report recommending the patient stay with the PRP. The therapist may be required to testify at a deposition or court. All of this raises the question: "What should be the role of the child's therapist when one of the parents has initiated a custody dispute and the court is intending to determine the patient's placement?" In our opinion, a mental health professional who is already involved in a therapeutic relationship should emphasize his role of helping the patient express his feelings, explore his fantasies, and deal with the events occurring in the child's life. In most situations it will be preferable for the therapist to emphasize the importance of his work with the child and to decline the invitation to become actively involved in the custody dispute. The therapist should confine himself to helping the patient deal with the process and outcome of the custody dispute and should not try to influence the outcome of the dispute by sending written reports and testifying.

The PRP and the attorney usually feel very strongly that the therapist is the ideal person to testify, since the therapist has come to understand the child patient so well and may be considered an expert in these matters. The therapist should take care not to succumb to the flattery. Although it looks superficially like the child's therapist is the perfect person to testify in a custody dispute, he really is not a good choice. For one thing, the therapist is almost certainly biased in favor of the custodial parent, even though he may try very hard to be neutral. His biases make his testimony almost worthless. Furthermore, there are risks involved in testifying. For instance, the confidential nature of the therapy will almost certainly be violated if the therapist testifies. Also, the therapist's testimony may adversely affect any future therapy with his client. The therapist's active role in influencing the outcome of the custody dispute is going to change the therapeutic alliance with the patient and also the relationship with the patient's parents.

Even when the therapist's opinion is adopted by the court, the effect on the therapy itself can be damaging. This phenomenon was illustrated at the beginning of this chapter in the case of Ms. Sears and Mr. Roebuck. In that case the psychiatrist was trying to be helpful, but his testimony was misinterpreted by the custodial parent, Ms. Sears. Since the doctor went to court and testified on behalf of Sally and Ms. Sears, they believed it meant Sally didn't have any more problems and ended her therapy. Her conditioned worsened and she had to be hospitalized.

Although it is usually best for the therapist to avoid active participation in these disputes, the therapist may wish to become involved indirectly by sharing verbal information with the independent mental health professional who is performing the custody evaluation. When the therapist is invited by a parent, an attorney, or a judge to participate actively and make recommendations regarding custody, the therapist can use the opportunity to explain the possible disadvantages of his taking that role. The attorney will probably have a better case if an independent psychiatrist supports his position rather than the potentially biased therapist.

The Basic Message

The most important thing for divorced parents and mental health professionals to remember is to be clear with each other regarding assumptions and expectations. If a parent really desires the therapist to testify on his or her behalf in court in two months, the parent needs to make his or her needs known at the beginning. If the therapist is working on the assumption that the confidentiality of the child's therapy is going to be protected from future legal proceedings, he needs to make it clear at the beginning.

Taking your child to a therapist is like taking your car to a garage. If you want the mechanic to check the brakes, you need to spell it out and make it clear what you are expecting. The mechanic can tell you whether he works on brakes. Likewise, the parent and the therapist need to be very clear with each other regarding what they see is the purpose of the therapy.

Chapter Eighteen
Divorce Mediation and Divorce Counseling

Cynthia Ryback and Howard Ryback were married for ten years. By the time they decided to divorce they both had plenty of ammunition and could have waged a substantial battle over custody of their two children, a 5-year-old girl and a 7-year-old boy. Cynthia was ready to allege that Howard had been alcoholic and was rude and offensive to her and the children when he was intoxicated. Howard had hired a private investigator, who was ready to testify Cynthia had stayed overnight with a male friend when she said she was visiting her sister. Both of the parents worked, although Howard, a supervisor in a laboratory, had a considerably higher income than Cynthia, who taught junior high school. They both felt very aggrieved and resentful. They had hired attorneys and were trying to get the money together for a prolonged court trial because they both were seeking custody of the children.

Cynthia's sister had heard about divorce mediation and explained it to Cynthia. She told Cynthia that going to trial would be extremely expensive, would be very upsetting, and might be damaging for the children. Cynthia was concerned she might not get the outcome she wanted through mediation, but she decided to call a mediator and get more information. The mediator was an attorney, who initially met with both parents at the same time. He also met with them individually, to help the parents define what they really wanted for themselves during and after the divorce. The mediator was knowledgeable about estate planning and taxes and was able to make some suggestions that saved Cynthia and Howard a good deal of money.

It became clear during the mediation process Howard was at a critical point in his career and was very interested in working hard in order to achieve a promotion. He really did not want to have the everyday responsibility for the children, but he wanted to be with them regularly. He wanted assurances that Cynthia was not going to take the children and move to another community. Since Cynthia was a teacher, she was much more available to supervise the children, especially during school vacations. They ultimately agreed on joint custody, with the children primarily living with Cynthia. They worked out a plan for how to handle the children's education, medical care, and religious upbringing. Since Howard had a higher income, he agreed to a reasonable amount of child support. Since Cynthia was working and she was allowed to remain in the family home, there was no alimony. She agreed to pay the mortgage. The mediator helped Cynthia and Howard agree to a formula for how the money would be distributed when the house was later sold.

The mediator was no magician, but he simply worked with the parents until there was a plan that both parties could live with. In order to make sure their rights were being protected, both parents took a draft of the proposal to their respective attorneys, who made some minor suggestions. They presented the final version to the judge, and Cynthia and Howard ended up with a relatively nontraumatic divorce. More importantly, the children did not suffer as much as they could have. A foundation was laid, on which the two separate families could build their future lives.

Mediation Is Not Therapy

Divorce mediation is a form of negotiation in which a trained individual, the mediator, helps two individuals who are divorcing work out the division of the marital property, parental responsibilities regarding the children, and other details related to the divorce. The purpose of divorce mediation is not to help the parents improve their relationship and get back together again. The purpose of divorce mediation is to assist the parents in achieving a relatively nonadversarial divorce. It is also intended to help the parents negotiate the arrangements for the children, including everything from schooling to bed times. In some states (such as California, Maine, New Mexico, Oregon, Tennessee, Wisconsin) an attempt at mediation is usually required before a divorce is granted.

Mediation is not the same as marriage counseling. In marriage counseling, the counselor is trying to help the couple communicate and have a better relationship. In divorce mediation, it is understood by everyone the marriage is over and the purpose of the meetings is to work out the terms of the divorce. *Divorce mediation is not the same as arbitration.* In arbitration, the ground rules usually provide that the neutral arbitrator will make the final decision regarding the dispute. In mediation, the neutral mediator does not make the final decision, but helps the divorc-

Books on Mediation

There is a long discussion of divorce mediation in the later edition of a book by Richard Gardner, *The Parents Book about Divorce* (Bantam Books, 1991).

For mental health professionals, there are several good books regarding divorce mediation, including: *Child Custody Mediation: Techniques for Mediators, Judges, Attorneys, Counselors and Parents,* by F. Bienenfeld (Authorhouse, 2002) and *The Handbook of Divorce Mediation* by S. Marlow and S. R. Sauber (Plenum Press, 1990).

Another book on this topic is by a married couple, John and Gretchen Haynes, who wrote *Mediating Divorce: A Casebook of Strategies for Successful Family Negotiations* (Jossey-Bass, 1989). There is a chapter on this subject in *Emerging Issues in Child Psychiatry and the Law,* which was edited by D. H. Schetky and E. P. Benedek (Brunner/Mazel, 1985).

The work of the parenting coordinator is discussed in detail in a book by Carla B. Garrity and Mitchell A. Baris, *Caught in the Middle* (Wiley, John & Sons, 1997).

ing couple arrive at a mutual agreement. Divorce mediation is a way for parents to communicate their needs to each other and to work out their disagreements. *Divorce mediation is not the same as divorce counseling.* The purpose of divorce mediation is to develop the parenting plan, which the court will endorse and make official. The purpose of divorce counseling, which occurs after the court has made the parenting plan official, is to help the parents implement the provision of the parenting plan on a day-to-day basis.

Mediation is facilitated by a neutral individual, who may be an attorney (who has additional training in psychological processes) or a mental health professional (who has additional training in legal issues). Divorce is a complicated process. If the mediator is an attorney, it may be necessary to use a psychiatrist or a psychologist to help the parents understand the needs of the children. If the parents cannot agree on the parenting of the children, the mediator may suggest they arrange for a neutral psychiatrist or psychologist to conduct a formal parental evaluation. The recommendation of the mental health professional would then be fed into the mediation process. On the other hand, if the mediator is a mental health professional, it may be necessary to consult with an attorney if there are unusually complicated legal questions, such as the tax implications of the division of the marital property.

Mediation is a good idea for divorcing couples who would rather save their money for the children's college education instead of spending it all in a four-day court battle. For mediation to work both parents have to be open minded enough to negotiate in a sincere manner. It is also necessary for each parent to have some respect for the point of view and the desires of the other parent, even though they may still be quite angry at each other. Finally, it is necessary for each parent to be reasonably trustworthy. We must remember it is difficult to trust someone who has broken your heart.

Even if an attorney is the mediator, almost always the divorcing individuals still have their own attorneys. This is important in order to protect the interests of the individual parents. Once the mediation is over, each party should ask his or her attorney to review the agreement. Occasionally, the attorneys discover something that seems unreasonable or unfair, which escaped the notice of their clients.

Parenting Plan

Another way to reduce the amount of fighting over the children and through the children is to develop a formal parenting plan, which was discussed in detail in Chapter Six. In general, a parenting plan is a detailed document that specifies all the issues regarding the children ahead of time, so it is less likely that arguments will occur later. The parenting plan would address the schedule the child has at each household, the plan for the child's education, the plan for medical care, the plan for religious training, and anything else that either parent might want to clarify. Most divorcing parents would need some help in developing a parenting plan.

Counseling for Divorced Parents

Divorce counseling refers to meetings divorced parents have with a mental health professional. Some writers call this "parenting coordination." For instance, the counselor or parenting coordinator may meet with the divorced parents together on a regular basis, such as once a month. We are not talking about meetings taking place prior to the divorce, as happens in divorce mediation, but meetings taking place after the divorce is over and when the parents are starting to lead their separate lives. The purpose of these meetings is to discuss how the two divorced parents can raise their children in a cooperative and reasonable manner. The most important aspect of this kind of counseling is simply establishing good communication between the parents. For instance, the counselor moderates discussions on topics such as: clarifying exactly what the parenting schedule is going to be over Thanksgiving vacation this year; figuring out how the youngster can be on his high school basketball team when he is living in two households; and comparing plans for birthday presents, so both parents do not get the son exactly the same 10-speed bicycle.

In working with divorced parents, it is necessary for the counselor to structure the meetings and keep the parents on task. It does not do anybody much good if the meeting degenerates into a session for digging up old grievances and angry back-biting. Divorce counseling is not the same as psychotherapy for the parents. It is simply a way to help the parents communicate and resolve issues rather than perpetuate the disagreements.

Sometimes the counselor who is working with divorced parents may want to see the children. For instance, suppose there is a great deal of conflict related to the visitations. The parents argue endlessly about how the father picks the children up at the wrong time; exposes them to the unsavory relatives in his extended family; fails to get them to Sunday school as he had agreed; and brings the children back dirty and hungry. The children, of course, end up in the middle of this dispute. The visitation happens every other weekend, so the therapist arranges a schedule for a meeting to occur once a week. During the week after the visitation, the therapist meets with the children as a group. They discuss how the last visitation went, what was good, what was bad, what was fun, and what they might prefer to do differently. They discuss some possible plans for the next visitation.

During the next week the therapist has a meeting with the two parents. After comparing notes about what happened during the previous visitation, they have a very specific discussion about the plans for the upcoming visitation. They clarify very precisely what the schedule and the various activities will be for the children. After that the visitation occurs; then the meeting with the children; then the meeting with the parents; and so on. The purpose of this form of counseling is not for the custodial parent to control what happens during the children's time with the noncustodial parent. The purpose is to have clear communication with the ultimate goal being the children will have a good relationship with both parents. This kind of counseling helps the children have a healthy and meaningful relationship with the noncustodial parent.

Therapists work with divorced families in many different ways—before, during, and after the divorce. In order to be successful, the parents should be clear about their needs and expectations from their therapists. Depending on the circumstances, the therapist may work primarily with the parents or primarily with the children. At times, therapists should be clever and creative in thinking out a treatment plan.

The mental health professional's role may be to provide therapy *or* to mediate *or* to do an evaluation for court. Above all, they need to be very clear about what their job is in each individual case. It is not possible to be everything for everybody.

Chapter Nineteen
Letting Go and Moving On

David and Jessica Tucker separated several times during their short but tumultuous marriage. When they were apart they missed each other. When they were together they disagreed on practically everything. They eventually divorced, but afterwards David and Jessica continued to see each other. When Jessica's garbage disposal stopped working, David came over and fixed it. When David was lonely, Jessica went to his apartment, where they fixed dinner together and sometimes had sex.

David became depressed and his performance at work deteriorated to the point where he sought help from his employee assistance program. The EAP counselor, a woman, met with David three times. He was very open with her and readily shared his memories, feelings, and opinions. In fact, he seemed to become overly attached to and dependent on the counselor. For example, he gave the therapist a small present. He had a few "anxiety attacks," when he phoned the therapist's office and answering service, in order to hear her reassuring voice. When he couldn't reach the therapist, David continued to call Jessica for support.

The therapist told David he needed to move on with his life. In particular, he and his former wife needed to be less dependent emotionally on each other: Jessica should find somebody else to fix her plumbing; David should find new friends. David decided to talk this over with a couple of men he knew at work, who were also divorced. The three men had similar experiences in their marriages and their divorces and found it helpful to compare their experiences. As time went on, David stopped worrying about Jessica's garbage disposal and he was no longer anxious and depressed.

This sounds like a simple story, but it was hard for David to think of himself as a divorced guy rather than a married guy. Once he did, he was able to let go of his relationship with Jessica and move on.

Sometimes it seems puzzling, that two people who can't stand each other still stay involved in each other's lives. Of course, it is under-

standable because intense interpersonal relationships are more complicated than simply "liking" or "not liking" somebody. Frequently people
have intense, but ambivalent, relationships. David probably felt very
attached to Jessica and very positive about some aspects of her personality, mind, and body. He presumably disliked or felt very negative about
other parts of Jessica. Likewise, Jessica may have had strong ambivalent feelings about David.

We think ambivalent relationships continue to tie people together
even after they separate and divorce. This is one reason why some people
have difficulty leaving a former spouse alone: they continue to be emotionally enmeshed, even though they know the relationship is destructive.

Having the Last Word

There are other reasons why divorced individuals continue to contact each other and punish each other. For example, they may feel
hurt, angry, and vengeful. Getting divorced is a very hurtful experience
in many ways. Getting divorced is like being told you have been a
failure for all those years, that a big chunk of your life has been a waste
of time. A person who knows you better than anyone else has rejected
you completely. Getting divorced is a serious blow to a person's pride
and ego.

The other big reason for anger is that one partner has taken steps
to terminate the marriage, so the other person feels wounded and enraged. It may be both parties have reason to feel abandoned and rejected, so they both are enraged at each other. Of course, once the divorce gets underway people do a lot of mean things to each other, so
there is even more reason to stay angry and continue the arguing. Both
parties want to have the last word, usually in a very big way. Add one
more component—disrupting the way the parents relate to their child—
and all-out war is declared.

Do This

There are many suggestions offered to people who find themselves
in this situation, who need to leave behind old relationships and move
on with their lives. This chapter contains some specific suggestions, but
we are sure anybody who has been through a difficult divorce can add to
this list.

- Deal with the feelings you are experiencing instead of denying them or burying them. That means: talk it out with family and close friends; cry a lot, at least for a while; get angry and call a few names if you need to.

- Find people who are in the same situation. You probably know them already, but never thought of them as people with whom you would socialize because they were divorced and you were married. Now that you are single again, you will probably enjoy spending some time with people who have had similar experiences. These people will probably become part of your personal support network.

- There is a chapter of Parents Without Partners in many cities. Call them. Since there are millions of single-parent households, they constitute a significant segment of the recreation market and vacation industry. There are campgrounds, resort hotels, cruises, and tours catering to single-parent families. For instance, the structure of Club Med resorts easily accommodates single-parent families—meals at large tables encourage mixing and meeting. Also, there are many group activities designed for children of different ages and adults of different interests.

- Renew contact with your parents and siblings. That is not to say you should go home to Mom and Dad and just sit there for the next three years, but you will probably enjoy being included on holidays and other special occasions.

- There are more formal ways of getting through rough times. Many churches and other community agencies have support groups and organized social activities for divorced individuals. It might seem hard to make the initial contact with such a group, but we are sure they will try to include you and help you feel comfortable. If you don't already belong to a church, join one.

- If you have children, they are even more reason why you need a support network. It is very hard to raise children all by yourself. Single parents get tired of watching *Barney* every day. Watching dinosaurs sing songs can get old if you don't get a break from it every so often. Single parents need the company of other adults in order to have conversations about grown-up subjects. These relationships will help your transition into single life.

- Focus on your plans for this week, next week, and the next couple of months. Write them down. Look at your list when you feel at loose ends. Don't dwell on the past. Develop a hobby. Go hiking—not by yourself, but with a group. There are hiking clubs in almost every city that organize weekend trips and adventures.

The Work of Judith Viorst

Judith Viorst is a prolific writer and a thoughtful person. Her work has ranged from children's books (*Alexander and the Terrible, Horrible, No Good, Very Bad Day*) to books about human nature and human development (*How Did I Get to be Forty and Other Atrocities*). Viorst wrote a book that might be of interest to couples who are married and/or divorced: *Grown-Up Marriage: What We Know, Wish We Had Known, and Still Need To Know About Being Married* (Free Press, 2002). She talks about marriage "as a problem we have to solve again and again," and gives abundant practical advice for individuals who are married for both the first and the second time.

In *Necessary Losses* (Simon & Schuster, 1986), Ms. Viorst merged her personal experiences as a daughter, mother, and wife with her training as a research graduate of the Washington Psychoanalytic Institute. She emphasized there are many, many losses and disappointments which we all encounter during every stage of life. Her point was that "these losses are a part of life—universal, unavoidable, inexorable. And these losses are necessary because we grow by losing and leaving and letting go." Ms. Viorst's message is particularly important for divorcing parents and their children.

- See if you can frame your divorce in the most positive way. It usually takes the form of something like: "I'm glad I finally got out of an unsatisfying relationship. Now I can work on being a better person and parent."

- Perhaps the hardest task to even think about is forgiveness. After time has passed, it should be possible to consider forgiving the persons who misused you in some way, whether it be your former spouse or other individuals—such as friends and relatives—who were on the periphery of the divorce. Forgiveness benefits both victims and perpetrators. If there is a perpetrator who experiences guilt, forgiveness is a balm for his or her unpleasant feelings. If there is a victim who still feels rage and vengeance many years after being injured, forgiveness helps to remove the burden. Both forgiveness and apologies work best when they are reciprocated, but reciprocation is not necessary to achieve personal peace.

Don't Do This

It should be clear to readers of this book that prolonged angry relationships between divorced parents are not good for the children. It is in your interests and also in the children's interests to call it quits, to leave the angry relationship behind, and to move on with your life. Better days are ahead. What makes it complicated is the prospect of raising the children together automatically means the divorced parents are going to stay in touch and communicate with each other. Since divorced parents cannot usually wave good-bye and move to another state, it is necessary to create a relationship that is civil, rather businesslike, and constructive from the point of view of the children. The best way to define such a relationship is to give some examples of unhelpful, destructive behaviors and later give other examples of constructive behaviors.

•   Don't rely on each other for all the little things as you did in the past. Find someone else to tune up your car, cut your hair, and do your income tax.
•   When the noncustodial parent has the child for visitation, he should not rely on the custodial parent to solve minor problems. If the child has a headache, for example, he should try to figure out for himself how many baby aspirins to give.
•   Don't start dating your former spouse or have sexual activities together. We suppose there are exceptions to this rule, since occasionally divorced individuals decide to get married again. However, this rule certainly seems like a good policy to follow most of the time.
•   Don't entertain the idea of organizing a happy Christmas together, with both of the divorced parents and both sets of grandparents all enjoying each other's company. Once again, we know there are exceptions because we have heard of families who are able to make this work. Most divorced families, however, should not try to recreate the good old days, which is supposedly being done for the sake of the children. Likewise, we suggest you don't try to spend a week at the beach with your ex-spouse and your kids.
•   Don't spend your energy and your financial resources on legal battles any more than necessary in order to protect your legitimate interests. That means you should not go back to court over and over if your only real purpose is to get revenge or to show you can have the last word by winning on some minor issue. You might win the

battle but lose the war because you will lose a meaningful relationship with your child.

There are notable exceptions to these do's and don'ts. There are occasional divorced couples who continue to have congenial, trusting, and mutually respectful relationships. They are able to plan Thanksgiving dinner together and may spend weekends together at activities which the parents and the children all enjoy. A couple of years ago there was a divorced couple in Arizona who raised two sons together. When the father's kidneys failed because of an inherited disease, the mother donated a kidney for his transplant. Couples like this are probably not reading this book, and they do not need to.

Constructive Communication

There are many times when divorced parents need to communicate and collaborate. Some examples may help define the difference between constructive communication and destructive behaviors.

• One of the themes of this book has been that divorced parents need to communicate about many aspects of child-rearing. On some items they need to reach agreement, such as the exact times of the parenting schedule. They may not reach agreement regarding many other issues—such as decisions regarding the child's education, medical care, and household rules—but they should at least listen to each other. Treat each other with respect. Both of you are responsible for raising your children.

• When there is continuing conflict between parents, we have suggested some aspects of the child-rearing should be done independently in order to reduce the fighting. For example, suppose both parents like to help their 14-year-old daughter, Nancy, with school work, but they give conflicting advice. Nancy gets frustrated and angry when she is caught between these well-meaning parents. So the parents agree to divide their efforts: the mother will help Nancy with her science fair project and leave the algebra alone; the father will go over Nancy's algebra homework, but will refrain from making suggestions about the science fair.

• There are occasions when divorced parents should make a strong effort to lay aside animosity, at least temporarily. Think about those important, singular times when children should feel proud of themselves and should feel good about their families—an example would be high school graduation. It seems to us this is one time divorced parents should be able to be in the same room at the same time. They are likely to have approximately the same thought, "It's great Johnny has made it to this point in his life."

•   Moving ahead a few years, what about the child's wedding? Advice columns—such as "Dear Abby," "Dear Margo," and "Ask Beth"—receive hundreds of letters about this topic. When the parents are divorced, who should be invited to the wedding? Who should be excluded? Who should give away the bride, the father or the stepfather? Who should help pick out the silver pattern, the mother or the stepmother? We realize there are no simple answers to these questions. If there were, Abigail Van Buren would simply write them all down and everybody could follow them. We do think a good general rule for weddings is for the divorced parents to put aside the mutual bitterness, probably started years previously, and create a beautiful day. Remember this is your child's day, not yours.

•   There may be other times a divorced person should enter into the affairs of his or her former spouse and go against the general rule of staying out of each other's lives. Suppose, for example, one of the parents has suffered an unusual crisis. Once there was a mother who found she had a serious form of leukemia. Although she and her ex-husband had waged several serious battles, especially over their children, the father sincerely wanted to be helpful. The father was a medical administrator and was able to locate a cancer research group that offered the mother specialized treatment. The man became rather involved with his former spouse's illness, but it seemed like the right thing to do.

"Letting go and moving on" can be a painful process, but it is part of many life experiences. This chapter is an echo of the three basic principles stated at the beginning of this book: children of divorce should have a good relationship with both parents; divorced parents should find ways to minimize the disruptions and make life as normal as possible for their children; and divorced parents and their children need to accept the inevitable losses and disappointments and to move on with their lives. Let us hope divorced parents and their children will be able to put their troubles into perspective and will be able to focus their energies on creating a brighter future rather than on reliving the past.

Chapter Twenty
Ten Steps

We live in a complex world and there are no quick and easy answers for most problems in our society. The same goes for raising children of divorced parents. Since life is full of twists and turns, it is good to stay on the main road with the central issues and not get side-tracked into petty, peripheral areas. Here are our suggestions for the most important things to remember about raising children of divorce.

Ten Steps for Raising Children in Divorced Families

1. Don't fight over the children, through the children, or in front of the children.
2. Children need to love and respect both parents.
3. Find ways to help the children have two homes, rather than one home and one hotel room.
4. Give appropriate consideration to the children's wishes.
5. Despite the divorce, find ways to create enduring family traditions.
6. Recognize the rights and responsibilities of both parents.
7. Both children and parents should develop and maintain interests which go beyond the divorce.
8. Both children and parents should move on with their lives. They should accept that life may not be exactly the way they would have planned it.
9. Don't try to do it by yourself—reach out and seek support from family, friends, church, and support groups.
10. When you need extra help, make use of professionals such as clergy and therapists.

Chapter Twenty-one
Resources

Since readers may wish to access additional resources, we have reviewed numerous websites on divorce-related topics available on the Internet. This chapter lists online resources with a brief synopsis of the issues highlighted in each website. These resources may be starting points for families seeking additional information regarding children of divorce. Of particular interest are those focusing on the concerns of grandparents and stepfamilies, which were addressed only briefly in this book. The following list, arranged alphabetically, is not all-inclusive. Also, every point of view expressed online is not necessarily completely correct or appropriate.

American Academy of Child and Adolescent Psychiatry
Facts for Families: Children and Divorce
http://www.parentshandbooks.org/factsfam.htm

This professional organization (AACAP) publishes many "Facts for Families" on a number of important topics. The "Facts for Families" includes "Children and Divorce" and also related issues such as "Children and Grief," "Children's Sleep Problems," "The Depressed Child," and "Stepfamily Problems." For instance, the material on divorce provides tips to help children and parents manage the challenges and stresses of conversations about divorce and information to help parents recognize signs of distress in their children.

Lee Borden, Attorney and Divorce Mediator
Divorceinfo: Here To Help You Survive Divorce
http://www.divorceinfo.com/

This website is a comprehensive divorce guide based on the author's extensive experience in law and divorce mediation. Mr. Borden provides interesting, helpful information and advice on various divorce-related financial and legal issues, including child support. This resource includes basic pointers on coping, managing your children during the divorce process, and addressing issues of anger, anxiety, and depression arising in divorce situations. There are discussions of miscellaneous other topics, including parental abduction, parenting at a distance, an adult child's divorce, "social divorce," and state-specific legal issues.

The Center for Divorce Education
"Children in the Middle"
http://www.divorce-education.com

The Center for Divorce Education is a nonprofit organization providing education on divorce-related issues and helping families deal with conflict centered about divorce. This website includes information about the Center's video-based educational programs designed to minimize children's anger toward the parents, withdrawal from family and friends, declining grades, and behavioral problems such as delinquency and substance abuse. The Center for Divorce Education sells an award-winning video, "Children in the Middle," which addresses the conflict children experience during separation and divorce, and "After the Storm," which addresses the conflict occurring after separation and divorce. There are links to PowerPoint presentations, research articles, and other divorce-related websites.

Divorce Central
Friends, Information, Expertise
http://www.divorcecentral.com/

This online service offers assistance and support for those at various stages in the divorce process. While numerous sections focus on legal matters, there is also a link, entitled "Parenting," that contains useful resources, such as "The Total Parenting Handbook." By clicking on this secondary link, you will discover a guide to raising children during divorce with chapters providing advice on custody such as: how to broach the topic of divorce with your children; how to help children with grief, anger, and rejection; and how to manage visitation. The Parenting link also contains a section on parents' frequently asked questions about raising children during divorce, a "Bill of Rights" for children of divorce, and links to additional websites on divorce-related parenting issues.

Family Education Network
Family Life/Divorce
http://life.familyeducation.com

This website addresses an extensive list of parenting topics, including a number of divorce-related issues such as legal and financial questions. The topics include the following: "Divorce: What To Tell Your Children," "Making Co-Parenting Work," "Age-Appropriate Visitation," "Managing Visitation in High-Conflict Situations," and "When Children Fight Visitation." There are discussions regarding dating during divorce, sharing custody, divorce and teens, behavioral problems and divorce, counseling for children, and many other topics. There is a highly frequented message board designed to allow members to share experiences as they go through the divorce process.

Focus Adolescent Services
Stepfamilies and Co-parenting
http://www.focusas.com/Stepfamily.html

Focus Adolescent Services is an Internet clearinghouse of information, resources, and support for adolescents and families dealing with numerous issues, including stepfamily relationships and divorce. This website provides comprehensive information for divorced parents and stepparents, and their families. For example, there are articles on challenges faced by stepfamilies, techniques for forming strong bonds in a new stepfamily, determining whether professional help is needed for children of divorced parents, and many other topics. There is a discussion, from both the legal and psychological perspectives, of parental alienation syndrome.

Helpguide
Mental Health Issues: Blended Families/Stepfamilies
http://www.helpguide.org/mental/blended_families_stepfamilies.htm

Helpguide is a large website that assists people with various problems and needs, including mental health issues. This website addresses the management of newly formed blended families or stepfamilies, and one of its best articles provides specific tips for making a stepfamily's transition period less challenging. The site also includes an adult section which provides information and ideas concerning financial agreements, living arrangements, resolution of feelings about the previous marriage, disciplining children, and anticipating changes in parenting and decision making. There is also a discussion of attachment problems experienced by children of divorce and how these problems affect a child's ability to adjust to the new family.

Helpguide
Mental Health Issues: Children and Separation/Divorce
http://www.helpguide.org/mental/children_divorce.htm

This Helpguide website provides general information regarding children and divorce. It contains many informative articles, including suggestions regarding notice to teachers when parents are divorcing, a description of the short-term and long-term effects of divorce, and identification of the potentially traumatic effects of divorce on children. There are suggestions for helping a child deal with anxiety and depression associated with the parents' divorce. Helpguide provides links to a number of related websites. Also, Helpguide itself is non-commercial.

Kids' Turn
A Unique Program for Families in Transition
http://www.kidsturn.org/

Kids' Turn is a nonprofit organization in San Francisco assisting children and parents in making their way through the divorce process. This website is unusual because it has separate sections for children and parents, which include interesting pages with questions and answers. The children's section also includes a guide to assist children in talking to their parents about divorce. There is an annotated list of books for children and adolescents of different ages. For parents, there are links to other helpful websites and information about workshops that take place in California.

Jennifer Lewis, M.D., and William Sammons, M.D.
Children and Divorce
http://www.childrenanddivorce.com/

Drs. Lewis and Sammons, pediatricians and authors of *Don't Divorce Your Children,* created this website to assist parents, children, and health professionals. Their advice and insights are based on twenty years of experience working with children and parents involved in divorce. This website includes examples, analyses, and advice on resolving different points of view among children and parents during and after divorce. There is a useful guide to developing a parenting plan, which includes defining the amount time spent with each parent, setting out a specific time and place for each handover, establishing guidelines for how parents can stay in contact with each other most effectively, defining vacation allocation of the children, and planning for last minute delays and cancellations.

Dawn Miller
The Stepfamily Life: A Column From Life in the Blender
http://www.thestepfamilylife.com/

This online editorial column features written accounts and advice for stepfamilies based on one stepmother's experiences. The website addresses many topics such as: a descriptive snapshot of stepfamilies in America today; advice on arranging holidays when a stepfamily is involved; how to survive Thanksgiving; suggestions for prioritizing family time while a member of a stepfamily; and helpful links to supplementary websites designed specifically for stepmothers, stepfathers, exspouses, children, and teenagers on issues ranging from custody to wedding planning.

National Center on Grandparents Raising Grandchildren
http://chhs.gsu.edu/nationalcenter/

This website is designed especially for individuals who are raising their children's children, and for professionals providing services for children and grandparents in grandparent-headed households. The website contains a databank of published articles and also an annotated bibliography on topics pertaining to grandparents raising grandchildren. The National Center provides educational programs and consults to agencies that serve this population. It also tracks legislation of interest to intergenerational families. The National Office publishes a newsletter and also maintains an online chat site for grandparents to share ideas about grandparenting.

National Family Resiliency Center, Inc.
Family Matters: Helping Families Cope With Changes Throughout
the Lifecycle
http://www.divorceabc.com

This Maryland-based organization created this website as a guide to
the educational and counseling programs that it provides for parents,
children, and professionals involved in the divorce process. There are
interesting articles on the following topics: "Child and Family Focused
Decision Making," "Thoughts From Judges About Divorce," "Thoughts
From Lawyers About Divorce," and "How Do I Know if My Child Needs
Counseling?" There is a "bookstore" with separate sections for parents,
children, and professionals. Also, the website has a useful section con-
taining answers to commonly asked questions on co-parenting, child
mental health issues, dating and remarriage, divorce-related facts and
figures, and definitions of legal terms.

National Fatherhood Initiative
Fatherhood Online
http://www.fatherhood.org

This website aims to enhance children's life experiences and wellness
by providing various services for fathers. The resources include a
downloadable brochure on how to be a better dad and access to the
Initiative's quarterly newsletter, *Fatherhood Today*. There is information about the Initiative's numerous educational programs, bookstore,
and links to additional websites pertaining to fatherhood.

National Stepfamily Resource Center
http://www.stepfamilies.info

This website is a good resource for stepfamily members seeking
community with others experiencing similar challenges. The website
includes: guides to books, articles, and other educational resources on
issues pertaining to stepfamilies; information on stepfamily law and
policy; a section on facts and frequently asked questions applicable to
parents and children in stepfamilies; and a list of support groups by
state with contact information.

Public Health Agency of Canada
Because Life Goes On . . . Helping Children and Youth Live With
Separation and Divorce
http://www.phac-aspc.gc.ca/publicat/mh-sm/divorce/toc_e.html

This in an elaborate website for separating and divorcing parents
that is provided by an agency of the Canadian government. There are
various sections addressing topics such as: suggestions for parents on
how to see the divorce from a child's perspective; communicating effectively with children about separation and divorce, including detailed tips
on how to be a good listener and how to gradually build on the children's
understanding over time; a good discussion on maintaining the child's
community of support, including family, daycare, school, and friends;
and clues to identify violence in the home during divorce.

University of Missouri Extension
Helping Children Understand Divorce
http://muextension.missouri.edu/xplor/hesguide/humanrel/gh6600.htm

This online brochure outlines divorce-related topics of discussion
and how to approach them with your children. Following a review of the
typical level of understanding about divorce held by children of different
ages, the brochure provides instructions for parents on appropriate
methods of addressing the feelings and ideas of children in each group.
This resource also contains a helpful guide for parents in the selection
of reading material to use in talking to their children about divorce and
addressing the needs of their children, an interesting overview of sibling relationships in divorced families, and discussions of many other
topics.

The University of North Carolina at Greensboro
Divorce Do's and Don'ts
http://www.uncg.edu/frc/Divorce%20Do.pdf

This downloadable pdf file was developed by a class at The University of North Carolina at Greensboro on "Theories and Principles of
Parenting." It is perhaps one of the most detailed lists of do's and don'ts
with respect to children in divorce situations. The website contains sections pertaining to children of different ages, including infants and toddlers, preschoolers, elementary school children, adolescents, and young

adults. There is also a separate section of special do's and don'ts for nonresidential parents and stepparents.

General Index

The index is divided into the general index, below, the Index of Family Vignettes, and the Index of Legal Cases. In the general index, the most important citations are in **bold.**

Mental health professionals, **153-160,** 163, 164
Michigan, 69
Miller, Dawn, 179
Missouri, 30, 59, 115, 181
Mother's Day, 82, 98, 101
Moving, **105-116**

National Center for Grandparents Raising Grandchildren, 179
National Family Resiliency Center, 180
National Fatherhood Initiative, 180
National Interdisciplinary Colloquium on Custody Law, 110
National Stepfamily Resource Center, 180
Neglect, **65-67**
New Mexico, 162
New Year's Day, 100
New York, 30
Noncustodial parent, 41, 43, 119
Non-primary residential parent (NPRP), 4, 8, 59, 119
Normalization, **9-10**
North Carolina, 181
NPRP, see non-primary residential parent

Oklahoma, 134, 149
Oregon, 58-59, 65, 162
Our Family Wizard, 86

Parenting plan, 16, 20, 29, **40-45, 46-54, 58-62,** 104, 117-118, 164, 179
Parenting time, 59, 60, **88-96**

Parents without Partners, 169
Pennsylvania, 103
Pickhardt, Carl E., 131
Preference of child, 38, 94-95
Presents, 85, 133
Primary caretaker, 33, 34, 36
Primary residential parent (PRP), 4, 8, 59, 119
Principles, 7, 139
Prison, 135, 137
PRP, see primary residential parent
Psychiatrists, 15, 35, 65, 66, 126, 152, 175
Psychologists, 15, 35, 65, 126, 140
Psychology, 2
Psychotherapy, see counseling
Public Health Agency of Canada, 181
Puccini, Giacomo, 40

Recreation, 124
Reed, Mary, 42
Relationship, parent-child, 7-9, 11, 12, 20, 24, 33, 35, 62
Religion, 10, 22, 52, 61, **102-104,** 118, 123-124, 134, 169
Relocation, **105-116**
Research, 155
Reverse custody dispute, 64
Ricci, Isolina, 42
Rights of children, 58, 59
Rights of parents, 61, **117-127,** 174
Rosh Hashanah, 99, 102

Sammons, William, 178
Sauber, S. R., 163
Schedule, 25, 60, 87, **89-92**

Index of Family Vignettes

Index of Legal Cases